ZOMBIE COMBAT SKILLS AND WARFARE STRATEGY

SEAN T. PAGE

ROSEN
PUBLISHING®

New York

This edition published in 2017 by:

The Rosen Publishing Group, Inc.
29 East 21st Street
New York, NY 10010

Additional end matter copyright © 2017 by The Rosen Publishing
Group, Inc.

Library of Congress Cataloging-in-Publication Data

Names: Page, Sean T.
Title: Zombie combat skills and warfare strategy / Sean T. Page.
Description: New York : Rosen Pub., 2017. | Series: Surviving zombie
warfare | Includes bibliographical references and index.
Identifiers: LCCN 2016002170
ISBN 9781499463897 (library bound)
ISBN 9781499463873 (pbk.)
ISBN 9781499463880 (6-pack)
Subjects: LCSH: Zombies--Humor.
Classification: LCC PN6231.Z65 P33 2016 | DDC 818/.602--dc23
LC record available at http://lccn.loc.gov/2016002170

Manufactured in the United States of America

Originally published in English by Haynes Publishing under the title: Zombie Survival
Manual © Sean T. Page 2013.

CONTENTS

ZOMBIE COMBAT AND WEAPONS

Most of us know what zombies are, the risks they pose to the living and how they can be killed or at least the theory of how to kill them. But now it's time to face up to some unpleasant facts.

Firstly, when the zombies take over humanity will no longer be top of the food chain. We will no longer be able to wander the streets confident that, unless savaged by an escaped tiger, we can safely handle any wildlife around. Sure, some folks will live in the wilds and will be wary of bears or snakes, but for most, an angry squirrel or moody rabbit holds no fear. This will all change after the zombie apocalypse.

Secondly, whilst you may have already realized that a single zombie can be clumsy, slow and not particularly well furnished in the brain department, it is nonetheless a potentially deadly opponent. Add to this that zombies frequently cluster and will often attack in 'hordes' then you soon realize the importance of understanding how to fight these creatures. They aren't going to leave you alone. There won't be any uneasy truce. They will come at you, your family and any survivors for as long as they are able.

This is why zombie combat should be central to any survival preparation, as sooner or later you will find yourself facing the walking dead.

ZOMBIE COMBAT

Every fighter has their own favorite technique or specialized weapon but the advice for beginners is to work your way methodically through the next few pages. Learn about **S.T.E.N.C.H.**, absorb the information about your enemy and practice both the unarmed and armed combat moves. Hopefully, you'll never face the dead without a weapon, but be prepared just in case and you'll have a better chance of staying alive. You should schedule zombie combat practice sessions for at least an hour a day.

Finally, remember to adapt these plans and tips to your own needs or those in your group. These are general guidelines, but you can always 'spice' them up with your own homemade weapons or adapt them so that others can defend themselves.

EVERYONE IN YOUR GROUP MUST BE ABLE TO FIGHT TO SOME DEGREE SO YOU COULD WELL END UP BECOMING A ZOMBIE COMBAT TRAINER BUT FOR NOW, READ ON AND TAKE NOTES

ZOMBIE COMBAT AND WEAPONS
YOUR LAST ZOMBIE KILL

Before considering combat and weapons any further, it is important to be clear that the majority of zombies killed by human survivors are killed by clubbing weapons. In a recent Ministry of Zombies survey more than 43% of zombie kills were made using a club-like weapon. We strongly advise that you always carry a clubbing weapon as a reserve to your main weapon.

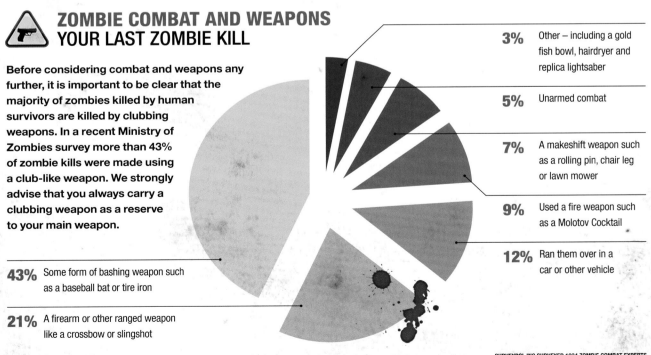

3% Other – including a gold fish bowl, hairdryer and replica lightsaber

5% Unarmed combat

7% A makeshift weapon such as a rolling pin, chair leg or lawn mower

9% Used a fire weapon such as a Molotov Cocktail

12% Ran them over in a car or other vehicle

43% Some form of bashing weapon such as a baseball bat or tire iron

21% A firearm or other ranged weapon like a crossbow or slingshot

SURVEYPOL INC SURVEYED 1034 ZOMBIE COMBAT EXPERTS

 **MINISTRY OF ZOMBIES**

THE WEAPONS OF A ZOMBIE
S.T.E.N.C.H.

SALIVA	Infected fluid – saliva and blood
TEETH	Sharp, jagged incisors
ENERGY	Consistent level of power
NAILS	Jagged weapons, like claws
CEASELESS	Won't stop, won't be scared off
HUNGER	Driven 100% by this hunger

Infected **SALIVA** dripping from the mouth. Where this is dry, it may be replaced by putrid bile or pus, which is just as deadly.

The dead have poor dental hygiene. **TEETH** tend to yellow under the zombic condition and endless gnawing on human bones frequently creates sharp and jagged incisors. Some zombiologists see this as nature's way of arming the carnivore!

The dead have seemingly boundless **ENERGY**. There are chemical and biological processes at work enabling zombie muscle mass to 'feed' on any fat within the corpse.

Whilst the finger **NAILS** do tend to grow after death, it is a slight retraction in the skin around the nail which gives it that dagger-like appearance. Again, endless scratching and foraging create sharp weapons riddled with infection and bacteria. With time, however, the nails may fall off.

A zombie is **CEASELESS** in its quest for human flesh. Zombie psychologists suggest that the dead see the living as having a warm golden glow around them. They are therefore obsessed with ingesting this 'lost life force'.

This **HUNGER** can never be abated. A zombie will cram living flesh into its mouth until its stomach cavity is at bursting point. How the dead break down food into energy is not yet fully understood. Few have the constitution to open up a zombie gut and review what's inside.

NOW CLOSE THIS BOOK AND TEST YOUR KNOWLEDGE: NAME THE KEY WEAPONS OF A ZOMBIE USING S.T.E.N.C.H.

ZOMBIE COMBAT AND WEAPONS

UNARMED COMBAT AGAINST THE DEAD

Make no mistake about it, no unarmed combat against the walking dead will ever be safe. Close combat with the infected is a dangerous business in which the living may be bitten or scratched at any time, not to mention the obvious health issues of tangling with a rotting corpse. It is advised that survivors carry at least a hand weapon at all times, be this a small hammer or even a large dagger.

However, there may be times when you do come face to face with the zombies and are unarmed. The following guidelines are designed for these occasions. Hopefully, you will never have to use them in combat, but ensure you know and practice the basic maneuvers. It could

mean the difference between you living to fight another day or becoming a buffet snack for a horde of the dead. Remember that unarmed combat must be supported by a comprehensive physical fitness training program. It's no use going for that lunge only to find that you pull a muscle or that you lack the strength to really drive a fist into that rotting zombie brain. The moves outlined over the next few pages do not demand any specific combat training, but they do require practice and that you achieve a reasonable level of fitness. You should consult a medical professional before starting any form of zombie unarmed combat training.

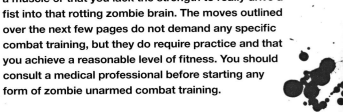

▶ DEFENSIVE MOVES

There are four classic defensive moves a fighter can use to defend a zombie attack: blocking, the neck grab, double-handed shove and the standard punch. There are hundreds of variants of these main types, but on the whole these four will be a powerful arsenal for those just looking to make a break for it at the first opportunity.

Ensure that you understand the three core principles before you start to practice these moves: your body must be in balance, your mind focused on the job in hand and remember that your objective is to create the room to escape – not to look like Bruce Lee in front of other survivors.

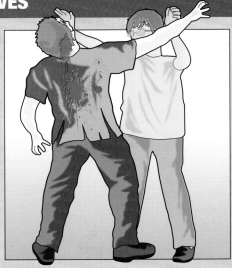

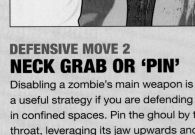

DEFENSIVE MOVE 1
BLOCKING

Remember a zombie has two primary vectors of attack – the grabbing claws and the snapping jaws. In close combat with the dead, you must always target these two areas as illustrated by our combatant in this figure. Here we are blocking both the oncoming jaw and the clubbing arm.

DEFENSIVE MOVE 2
NECK GRAB OR 'PIN'

Disabling a zombie's main weapon is a useful strategy if you are defending in confined spaces. Pin the ghoul by the throat, leveraging its jaw upwards and away from your holding arm. Squeezing the corpse's throat will do no damage and may lead to the head collapsing forward. Also, always uses your spare hand to deal the 'death blow'. Remember, the zombie will still have its arms.

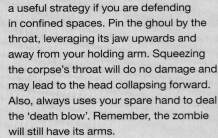

THE CORE PRINCIPLES

Written down over 1,000 years ago, they still form the foundation of all self-defense against the dead.

THE BODY IS BALANCED
You should be fit, steady and standing on both feet.

THE MIND IS STEADY
Your mind must not succumb to panic. Your mind should be clear and braced for combat.

CREATE THE ROOM TO ESCAPE
Remember that the objective is to disable the dead to create space for your escape.

> **ONLY THE SUICIDAL WOULD ENGAGE THE DEAD IN PROLONGED HAND-TO-HAND COMBAT. IT IS LIKE A MAN FIGHTING AGAINST THE TIDE. SOON, HE WILL BE OVERCOME BY EITHER THEIR TEETH OR THEIR BLOOD.**

TZU SAN LEE,
JOURNAL OF A YUNNAN PROVINCE ADMINISTRATION, 1220

In modern terms, you must be combat-ready at all times. You must be fit and agile, with your mind fully focused. Remain cool and calm in action – if you are to survive, you need to move like a warrior. If you find yourself without a weapon, have a good look around you – most locations will yield at least some items you can use as hand-held weapons.

DEFENSIVE MOVE 3
DOUBLE-HANDED SHOVE

This is a simple but effective move to give you that extra room to make your escape. It involves the fighter taking a firm footing, then pushing both arms forward towards the zombie, with hands out flat to meet the creature. The target area should be the upper chest and the force should cause the zombie to fall backwards or at least be pushed away. Do not attempt this move on any zombie that appears to be in an advanced stage of decay or with an obvious chest wound or you could end up with your hands buried, or worse, stuck in the chest cavity of the ghoul.

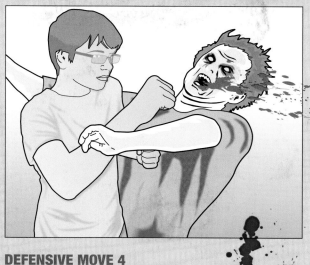

DEFENSIVE MOVE 4
STANDARD PUNCH

Unless you are wearing strong protective gloves, a punch to a zombie should always be delivered to the side of the jaw or, if the target is unclear, the side of the head. A direct punch to the front increases the risk of your fist being punctured by the ghoul's sharp, jagged and infected teeth. A powerful swinging punch from the side can take the lower jaw off, rendering the zombie unable to bite down. Never punch a zombie in the mid-section – the creature will not be wounded and it is likely to bury its face in your body.

ZOMBIE COMBAT AND WEAPONS

THE DIFFERENCE IN FIGHTING THE DEAD

There are some important differences when facing a zombie in unarmed combat and those experienced in martial arts or self-defense sometimes struggle to fully grasp this rule change. To be clear, traditional combat techniques used against the living need to be adapted for use against the walking dead. In general, the martial arts and any intensive fitness training will provide a good foundation for unarmed combat against zombies, but it is often the case that experienced martial artists do not appreciate the great difference between battling a living opponent in a training dojo and taking on several ravenous zombies on a street corner.

▶ Vulnerable points on a human, such as solar plexus, groin or bridge of the nose are not appropriate to zombies who have no feeling in these areas.

▶ A classic low karate kick may work to disable a living opponent but against zombies it will send the ghoul forward, its jagged nails outstretched. The most likely outcome is a 'raking' by which the dead drag their infected nails down you as they fall.

▶ The dead obey no rules other than the one that makes them want to feast on your flesh. Some martial artists come from such a disciplined background that they forget a zombie has no honor and feels no mercy or pain.

▷ BASIC UNARMED COMBAT MOVES

There will be occasions when blocking is simply not enough. You may need to seriously impair or damage your attacker. There are four basic moves in a typical zombie self-defense program: the Queensberry blast, the upper cut, the 'Captain Kirk' and the low knee kick and dash.

Three of these moves are made using the arms as they are traditionally the easiest for beginners to master without losing their balance and are most instinctive. We start with a variation of the standard punch which is a core move in any unarmed combat defense program.

BASIC MOVE 1
QUEENSBERRY BLAST

The fighter must adopt a classic boxer stance, with one leg slightly forward. The Queensberry Blast is a natural combination of two jabs to the upper half of the zombie head. The punches should land in rapid succession and it is likely that the force will lead the corpse to stumble backwards. It is a low-energy move that can be useful where the fighter lacks the strength to take out the zombie with one punch.

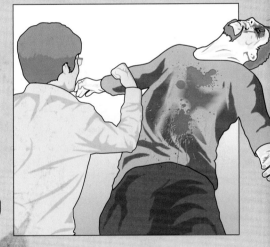

BASIC MOVE 2
UPPER CUT

Similar to a standard punch, this upward sweeping blow can prove fatal to a zombie when delivered with enough force. The user shifts onto one side, swings an arm back and delivers the punch directly underneath the chin, forcing the corpse's head to whip back. It can be a powerful punch to disable a zombie with, but sometimes it leaves the dead with a shattered row of sharp teeth – something they will be thankful for as it makes it easier to pierce through living flesh.

- ▶ However, a kick to the knee or gouging of the eyes can still 'damage' a zombie's movement or sight. Just be aware that pain and any disability will have no impact on the dead's desire to feed on the living. If these walking corpses get the chance, they will munch down hard on your flesh.
- ▶ Classic self-defense and martial arts holds rely on leveraging an opponent and using pain to restrict their movements. Few of these techniques will work on the dead.

IF YOU HAVE BEEN TRAINED IN ANY COMBAT TECHNIQUES, THE BEST ADVICE IS TO FORGET WHAT YOU HAVE LEARNED. MANY TRADITIONAL MOVES WILL BE SUICIDAL AGAINST THE DEAD.

BASIC MOVE 3
THE 'CAPTAIN KIRK'

Supposedly taught to William Shatner by an ex-Army Ranger stuntman, his trademark double-handed punch is particularly effective against the dead when delivered from behind. With force and making contact with the mid-back section, it will drive the zombie face down to the ground, making for an easy stamping target. Delivering a double-handed punch to the front is similar but involves whipping the hands out of harm's way much quicker. Shatner himself always preferred two punches, one to the middle then a knock down to the back of your opponent.

BASIC MOVE 4
LOW KNEE KICK & DASH

The most useful move in combat against the undead is the low knee kick, which will temporarily disable the zombie and enable you to make your escape. The move is most effectively delivered when the kick strikes the side of the knee, almost in a stamping motion. Be especially wary of the corpse's direction of fall and remember that this will not disable the ghoul's snapping jaws. This move will leave an active crawler behind even if you manage to shatter the knee joint. Remember, this is not a kill move – it's a basic move designed to give you time to make a run for it.

ZOMBIE COMBAT AND WEAPONS

NO HEROICS

Where you can make a run for it, do so – there is nothing heroic about hand-to-hand combat with the dead. But if you're going to stand your ground, never attempt to face the undead in unarmed combat if there is a weapon to hand. Grab what you can and use it! Here are a few examples you may not have considered.

ON THE SUBWAY OR TRAIN?

Use the train doors to crush the zombie's head. If they are already in the subway or train car, grab a shopping bag and swing it round Wild West style. Kick the zombie off the platform towards an oncoming train. Of course, this would delay your trip.

LINING UP AT THE SUPERMARKET?

Throw rubbing alcohol or lighter fluid on the zombies and then skilfully flick a match. Saving that, a frozen turkey to the head is a powerful clubbing weapon. If you are a sports fan and have the skills, you may be able to take a zombie down by throwing a can and hitting the ghoul in the head.

IN A BOOKSTORE?

Throwing piles of hardcover books will knock the dead over from a distance. Try to use the coffee table books as they tend to be thicker.

▷ ADVANCED UNARMED COMBAT MOVES

Once a fighter has mastered the basic moves in combat, there are hundreds of more advanced techniques that can be learned. Some will take months of practice, but many offer breathtaking alternatives to use in action, with moves that can save lives and take out multiple zombies at a time. Start your training by learning basic kick moves. A simple kick to the chest will often send a zombie tumbling to the ground, but ensure that you have the balance to stay on your feet before trying to kick any higher – remember the core principles of combat against the undead – balance, clear mind and room to escape.

ADVANCED MOVE 1
HIGH HEAD KICK

Much maligned in normal self-defense for leaving its proponent vulnerable to counter attack, against the undead a well-placed kick can knock a zombie down, and in the cases of extremely desiccated creatures take their heads off completely. The user must be fit and limber to use this move. Pulling a muscle in unarmed combat against the dead will reduce the principal advantage you have over the zombies, which is your speed.

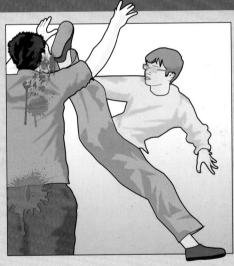

ADVANCED MOVE 2
THE 360 TORNADO KICK

This move is specifically designed to knock down multiple undead opponents. The fighter swings their legs back before jumping high into the air to deliver their first blow. Using the momentum of the swing, the leg should then follow round, hitting one target after another in a circular motion. All of the momentum will be driven into your lead or landing leg to deliver the multiple blows. It can appear as if the fighter is 'floating' so this is one impressive move.

ZOMBIE COMBAT AND WEAPONS
THE SOUTHERN PRAYING MANTIS

This is a complete system of combat specifically designed for use against zombies. Thought to originate in the monasteries of the Wudang Mountains in China, this highly skilled art has an emphasis on rapid hand work and short kicks, many of them low. Little is known of this art in the West and it has tantalized martial arts fanatics around the world to hear of the moves such as Sarm Bo Jin, which literally means 'Three Step Arrow'. The few accounts we have compare the style to that of a graceful street fighter. If you can obtain training in this art then this is the perfect preparation for the zombie apocalypse. According to Chinese zombie experts, an elderly monk known only as Zhang Sanfung is the only living master of the Southern Praying Mantis.

REMEMBER THE CORE PRINCIPLES OF COMBAT AGAINST THE UNDEAD – BALANCE, CLEAR MIND AND ROOM TO ESCAPE

ADVANCED MOVE 3
DOUBLE DROP KICK

This is an advanced move that requires great agility, but it can deliver a powerful, even knockout, blow to a zombie. Users require a good run up followed by a flying leap towards the undead opponent. The two feet should land squarely on the chest and the force will send the ghoul tumbling backwards. A disadvantage of this technique is that the user is left prone and vulnerable on the floor for a few seconds. However, it can be most useful if a zombie is threatening multiple targets and you just need to get the creature well away, for example from children or wounded.

ADVANCED MOVE 4
THE AERIAL

This is basically a forward somersault, normally with hands. The kicking leg swings over the top and lands with incredible force on the top of the zombie. The trick is to kick up your back leg as you take off. As your body gains velocity, the leg flips forward causing the body to flip and the foot to come down with skull-crushing force. This is really a show move and any slip-ups will leave you prone to counterattack by your ghoulish opponent. However, pull it off and you will appear to any watching survivors to be the post-apocalyptic equivalent of Bruce Lee.

ZOMBIE COMBAT AND WEAPONS

ARMED COMBAT AGAINST ZOMBIES

Within weeks of a major zombie outbreak, the walking dead will outnumber the living by thousands to one. Survivors will no doubt become experts with their trusty hand weapons, but they will need some serious firepower if they are to even up the odds.

Studies have shown that survivors do not need access to firearms to survive the walking dead. Preparation, training and a survivor mentality can be enough to get you through. So, guns are not an essential aspect of preparation for the zombie apocalypse, and in any case in most parts of the world their ownership and use is heavily regulated. However, someone 'tooled' up and trained will be in a stronger position to fend off the dead.

> ⚠️ **IMPORTANT**
>
> ALWAYS REMEMBER THAT THE OWNERSHIP AND USE OF FIREARMS IS CONTROLLED BY LEGISLATION. ZOMBIE SURVIVAL IS ABOUT KEEPING YOURSELF AND YOUR FELLOW SURVIVORS ALIVE, NOT CREATING HASSLE FOR THE POLICE. ALL ZOMBIE SURVIVALISTS MUST ENSURE THAT THEY ADHERE TO ALL LEGAL REQUIREMENTS AND ARE FULLY TRAINED TO USE THE WEAPONS DESCRIBED IN THIS MANUAL. BE LEGAL. BE SAFE. BE TRAINED.

A PRIMER ON ZOMBIE KILLING WITH GUNS

HANDGUN

RANGE: **SHORT**
WEIGHT: **LIGHT**

Close-range head shots below 33 feet (10 m). Ideally, every fighter should be equipped with a handgun. They can be secured safely around the belt.

RIFLE/ASSAULT RIFLE

RANGE: **MEDIUM**
WEIGHT: **MEDIUM**

Perfect for sweeping small hordes of the dead and mobile firing. Every patrol or foraging team should be equipped with at least one rifle.

SHOTGUN

RANGE: **SHORT**
WEIGHT: **MEDIUM**

Ideal for in-building combat or bursts into tightly packed hordes. It is good practice to have a 'shotgun fighter' covering your foraging group when inside buildings.

MACHINE GUN

RANGE: **MEDIUM–LONG**
WEIGHT: **HEAVY**

Perfect for sweeping advancing hordes and defending survivor settlements from a fixed firing position.

REMEMBER: A ZOMBIE SURVIVALIST USES THE RIGHT GUN FOR THE RIGHT JOB AND A HEAD SHOT WILL PUT A ZOMBIE DOWN FOR GOOD

DON'T SHOOT YOURSELF
Even if this doesn't kill you, you'll be slowed down and the scent of blood will attract hordes of the dead.

NEVER, EVER POINT GUNS AT HUMANS
Loaded or not, never point a gun at another human being unless you are in combat. For the untrained idiot, there's more chance that you'll shoot a fellow survivor as you do your Robert De Niro impressions.

NEVER FIRE OFF ALL OF YOUR AMMUNITION
A full clip can make the gun amateur feel very powerful but on fully automatic it can empty in just a few seconds. Don't forget to maintain your weapon. No matter which gun you use, all require care and maintenance. Imagine yourself trying to reload your Grandad's antique flintlock musket with the ghouls bearing down on you.

DON'T BE A POOR SHOT
It is no exaggeration to say that only an accomplished marksman will be able to get the kind of head shots needed to take down a zombie. Others may be able to hit limbs and slow down the dead, but more often than not inaccurate shooting under very stressful conditions will put them on the menu.

DON'T BECOME OVER-CONFIDENT
Firearms have that effect on people. Just remember, no matter how many handguns or rifles you have, the dead only need a small chance to bite or scratch you and it's game over, man. To paraphrase Darth Vader, do not over-estimate the power of the technology you have created.

HANDGUNS ─────

More common than larger firearms, many police and security forces around the world are armed with side arms. They are generally light with little recoil and are ideal for close combat against the dead. The Beretta 92F is an ideal balance of firepower, reliability and weight, making it the favoured handgun choice of many zombie survivalists. However, there are hundreds of different guns out there so review your options carefully and remember that in terms of maintenance, spare parts and ammunition, it is easier if your group is equipped with the same or similar models.

FRONT SIGHT · **BARREL** · **REAR SIGHT** · **HAMMER** · **SAFETY** · **MUZZLE** · **TAKE-DOWN LEVER** · **TRIGGER GUARD** · **TRIGGER** · **GRIP PANEL** · **MAGAZINE RELEASE** · **MAGAZINE**

BERETTA
92F 9MM

EXPERIENCE COUNTS

In a Ministry of Zombies field study at three gun clubs in the USA, only 30% of experienced shooters achieve a 'kill shot' on zombies at 100 feet (30 m). To those trained in the use of firearms, the kill figures below may look lower than one might expect from a group of experienced shooters. However, during this live-fire exercise, combat conditions were simulated to disrupt and distract. For example, loud klaxons were played and targets moved, simulating a real zombie. This field study confirmed that even the most experienced shooters struggled to make a kill shot with a handgun at over 65 feet (20 m). The lesson is therefore that a pistol is a close-range weapon of last resort except for a very skilful shooter with cast-iron nerves.

RANGE	% 'KILL SHOT'
165 feet (50 m)	10%
130 feet (40 m)	13%
100 feet (30 m)	30%
65 feet (20 m)	45%
32 feet (10 m)	71%

This field study was completed in April 2012, involving 167 shooters, all with at least two years' experience.

HANDGUN INSTRUCTIONS

1 Always read the product manual. A firearm is not a DVD player and you do need to know how to use all of its functionality against zombies.

2 Keep it locked and unloaded when not out and about in zombietown.

3 Learn how to reload properly and how to complete the exercise under time pressure. Getting a magazine jammed with any firearm could get you killed.

4 When in combat, draw your weapon and ensure that the safety is off. Hold the gun steadily and be aware of nervous trembling, which could disrupt your shot.

5 Identify your target. Know the signs of a zombie. A warning may be used if appropriate.

6 Your stance should be your strongest foot in front with your pelvis turned 45 degrees towards the attacking zombie.

7 Breathe slowly and aim at the face of the zombie. Most panicking fighters tend to shoot high so a good strategy is to aim for the lower neck or torso. Pull the trigger in a smooth motion.

8 If your target has been dispatched, move on. If not, complete a stamp to the head with your boot to destroy the zombie. Be aware that the loud crack of a pistol or any firearm will attract more of the dead, so each time you use your gun, balance carefully the options you have. Could you, for example, take out the zombie with a clubbing weapon instead?

CLOSE-RANGE HANDGUN SHOT

If they have the weapons, every survivor should be armed and trained with a handgun for emergency self-defense. It may be used when noise is not an issue or a fighter just needs to 'get the job done'. The ideal distance for the average shooter is less than 32 feet (10 m) – any more and accuracy will suffer. The fighter must pause for a few seconds and regulate their breathing before smoothly squeezing off one round. A full-face shot from this distance will take out a zombie in more than 87% of cases, depending on the gun.

ZOMBIE COMBAT AND WEAPONS

SHOTGUNS

Shotguns are the ideal firearm for the zombie apocalypse. The barrel of these flexible weapons is smooth as opposed to 'rifled' and they are designed to deliver powerful blasts at short range. Most will fire ball bearings or pellets, and there are literally hundreds of variations, but modern semi-automatic shotguns such as the Franchi SPAS-12 are pretty much unbeatable as zombie-busting weapons. The tactics below are designed for use with modern shotguns. If you find yourself armed with your Grandad's old hunting double-barrel then you will need to adapt the techniques. Any shotgun will be of use, so the capabilities of the weapon just need to be understood.

CENSORED
IMAGE DEEMED TOO SHOCKING FOR PUBLICATION

TACTIC 1
CONTROLLED SPRAY

A controlled spray is the maintenance of ongoing but regulated fire into a horde of zombies. Typically, it is used when retreating back down a corridor while being chased by significant and tightly packed numbers of the dead. The shooter effectively walks backwards, spraying various angles of fire into the oncoming horde and switching between low and high shots. In some cases, the shooter will actually shout 'low' when aiming into the legs – the ghouls hit by the spray aren't necessarily killed but do stumble and fall, causing an obstruction to those that follow. For the other shot, the shooter will shout 'high' – this is the killer head shot designed to thin out the zombies. Behind the shotgun shooter is a fighter pulling them slowly backwards and directing them to the exit. This move requires experience, discipline and a trusted partner as the shooter is entirely occupied with maintaining the field of fire while they are led by their partner to safety.

TACTIC 2
THE SHOTGUN SPLATTER

This is an extravagant special move that involves putting the barrel of the shotgun into the mouth of the zombie and blasting upwards. This has become something of a cult move amongst seasoned zombie killers and they take great pride in measuring the distance of the splatter after a shot.

It is important to wear eye protection as the spray is infected, but this is a morale-boosting move for the gung-ho zombie warrior. Equally, it is important to ensure that any audience is well out of range of any splatter and ideally behind you, as they enjoy your shotgun showboating. As extravagant as this move may first appear, it is still one that guarantees a solid kill every time. Just ensure that the zombie doesn't push the barrel down its throat in any effort to reach your fingers – this would not be a good way to become infected!

FRANCHI
SPAS-12

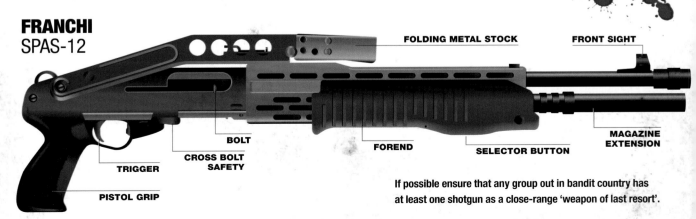

FOLDING METAL STOCK

FRONT SIGHT

BOLT

CROSS BOLT SAFETY

TRIGGER

PISTOL GRIP

FOREND

SELECTOR BUTTON

MAGAZINE EXTENSION

If possible ensure that any group out in bandit country has at least one shotgun as a close-range 'weapon of last resort'.

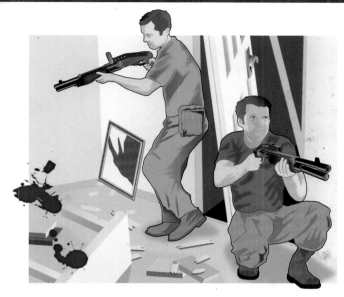

TACTIC 3
THE ROOM CLEARER

Clearing a building full of zombies is a nerve-wracking and dangerous process, particularly if you are unsure of its layout and the lights are out of order. However, with the right training, two experienced zombie fighters armed with shotguns can make good progress clearing locations of the dead. The first step is to have one fighter on each side of the door. They are both silent and one whistles or makes a noise to attract any ghouls within. They wait for a few seconds listening for any response. One then enters while the other covers. The fighter in the room checks each corner and any obstructions from the crouched position and shouts 'First Zombie Clear!' to indicate that the first sweep has been completed. The second fighter then enters and completes a secondary sweep covered by the first fighter, shouting 'Second Zombie Clear!' once the scan is complete. Shotguns are the perfect weapon for this kind of work.

> ## SHOTGUN TOP TIPS

> ▶ Wear protective clothing including face, eye and ear protectors. The blast in a confined space can be very noisy and there is a good chance of infected material splattering everywhere.
> ▶ Practice swinging the shotgun into the firing position in front of the mirror. Use hard-man phrases to add to the impact such as 'You lookin' at me?' or 'Do you feel lucky punk?'
> ▶ Remain calm in close combat. An overrun home can be a chaotic place. Always identify your target before shooting, don't just open fire at the first movement.
> ▶ When pointing the gun, always focus on the target, not the barrel of the gun. With a shotgun, it's a question of pointing not aiming.
> ▶ The shotgun is a zombie survival weapon rather than a 'kill as many as you can' weapon. It is ideal to use during a fighting retreat in an overrun location or wherever zombies are packed tightly together.
> ▶ If you are armed with an old-fashioned double-barrel or have limited shells then give the weapon to one of your most trusted fighters with the brief that they should only open fire when the team is in danger of being overrun.

WHY ZOMBIES DON'T LIKE SHOTGUNS

Below is an illustration of a shotgun blast slowed to 1/1,000,000th of a second. The wadding separating and splitting of the shell into 'pellets' can be seen clearly. It's these projectiles, which scatter over a decent range, that do the damage. It only needs a few to rip into a zombie skull and do the necessary damage.

STAGE 2

As the shell breaks up and splinters, you have a good balance of impact and shrapnel to do some serious damage. Even a small fast moving ball bearing can take down a zombie.

STAGE 1

Apart from a deliberate move such as the Shotgun Splatter, you should never hit a zombie this close. The shell has yet to splinter and there is a danger that the first zombie takes the full force of the blast.

STAGE 3

The most likely outcome of a shotgun blast from 50 feet (15 m) upwards is to knock any zombies in the fire zone to the floor. Depending on the weapon, the power of the shot can be significantly reduced at ranges of above 100 feet (30 m).

ZOMBIE COMBAT AND WEAPONS

MACHINE GUNS

Light machine guns are typically designed to be fired by a single mobile survivor whereas medium and heavy guns typically are meant to be fired from a fixed position, say on a tripod, or rely on a second survivor to feed in a belt and for general support. Whatever the type, in the hands of a skilled operator and in the right position, these weapons can inflict some awesome destruction on advancing zombie hordes.

MACHINE GUN TACTICS FOR BEGINNERS

To defend against zombie attack, machine guns are best placed at key points in your home, for example, in prepared machine gun pits with clear views and overlapping fields of fire. The ideal strategy is to draw in the dead by offering a direct route to get to their feast. Obstacles and pits can be used to tangle and ensnare the walking dead, but the main objective is to drive them into a 'cone of death' where both gunners can concentrate their fire on a wall of rotting flesh.

Crews should be made up of the most experienced survivors. They must be disciplined enough to hold their fire until a horde attack and even then to maintain a controlled-burst fire pattern as the dead advance. Most machine guns will overheat under sustained firing so their role will be to thin out the zombie ranks as they approach. Machine guns in fortified emplacements should always be supported by other more mobile fighters.

If you have a spare machine gun, you may consider mounting it on the back of a pickup truck. This can offer your forces mobile fire support plus a cool 'bandit king' look, which will put off most human raiders. A white or red pickup truck is best for this. Black or silver ones just look cheap and will appear like you're trying too hard.

M60
MACHINE GUN

FRONT SIGHT

BARREL

CARRY HANDLE

REAR SIGHT

COVER

GAS SYSTEM

HAND GRIP

FEEDWAY

PISTOL GRIP

SHOULDER STOCK

BIPOD LEG

Did you know that the M60 machine gun can fire well over 500 rounds per minute with a muzzle velocity of 930 yards (830 m) per second and to a range of over 1,094 yards (1,000 m)? That's a lot of shredded zombies if you can get your targeting right.

FIREARMS ARE NOT FOR EVERYONE

AVAILABILITY

When the zombie attack comes, it should be noted that laws concerning firearms use and ownership mean that weaponry will not be readily available to many fighters, especially in most of Europe. The chart below provides some country-by-country information on firearm availability and has been prepared by a panel of international firearms experts and the G.A.G.M. (Global Association of Gun Manufacturers), though the comments are all our own work. However, we would not advise people to move to a particular country purely because of availability of firearms. To calculate a truer 'zombie survival index' you must factor in conditions such as population density, the capacity of the local armed forces and geographical location. When these are included, countries such as Canada and Australia are good options for survival. People in the UK and Japan, though, will have a much tougher time of it.

AMMUNITION AND SPARE PARTS

Any guns in your group are only as good as the training people have had, how long the ammunition lasts and how the weapons have been maintained. If you have gathered a large survival group around you, it may be an idea to create a central armory where stocks can be managed and weapons serviced. A knowledgeable expert can also help offer training and ensure that the right weapon is taken for the right job. For example, one survivor may be jealously clutching their prize shotgun as they do guard duty, but the weapon could be of more use to a team engaged in foraging operations. If you are preparing to survive with an extended team, it makes sense to agree a list of preferred weapons rather than have everyone picking from the thousands of variants available. The AK-47Z is ideal if you can get hold of a small batch and we strongly recommend at least one M60 machine gun.

COUNTRY	GUNS PER 100 RESIDENTS	RANK	EXPERT ANALYSIS
UNITED STATES	88.9	1	Almost a gun for every fighter. Yee-hah!
SWITZERLAND	46.3	3	Neutral, ?!?! – the Swiss are ready to rock and they have the cheese to back it up.
IRAQ	37.3	8	Near war conditions may be a downer on your survival plans. Don't book an airline ticket just yet.
NORWAY	33.4	11	Fjords, wonderful patterned sweaters and enough guns to start a small war. A perfect balance.
GERMANY	30.4	15	You cannot help but be disappointed. They used to have a huge arms industry but it all went so very wrong.
MONTENEGRO	25.1	21	If we knew where this was, we would pass comment. It's bound to be hot. Probably nice food as well.
ANGOLA	17.6	34	Disappointing. Very disappointing. It's like they can't be bothered.
BRAZIL	8.3	75	Perfect jungle hiding locations but no guns and lots of snakes.
UNITED KINGDOM	5.5	88	Battling the dead with a cricket bat and an unarmed police force. Classy but ineffective in terms of guns.
JAPAN	So low it doesn't show up...	171	What happened Japan? You used to be cool. Now all you have is Manga and no guns.

THE BOW

Forget running round the forest in green tights and a small leafy hat; a modern bow is a deadly weapon in trained hands and one that could enable you to deal quickly and silently with those pesky ghouls that just won't stop hanging around. Obviously a head shot is the ideal, but this won't always be easy on a moving target or in the heat of battle. The next best target is the torso, not only because of its size but also because it is perfect for pinning a zombie to, say, a door or wall.

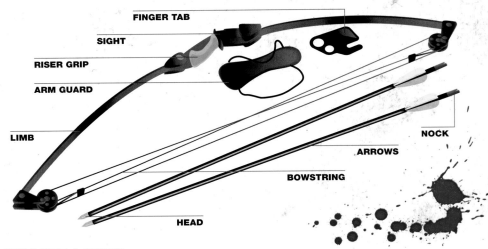

FINGER TAB
SIGHT
RISER GRIP
ARM GUARD
LIMB
NOCK
ARROWS
BOWSTRING
HEAD

WHY USE A BOW?

A bow is a flexible shaft, which is drawn back via the tension in a bow string. It is designed to fire projectiles known as arrows. There are hundreds of different types, but most modern bows are of strong, flexible fiberglass construction and come with a range of extras from stabilizing systems to telescopic sights. The main advantage of a bow is its ability to 'kill' the walking dead silently, without giving away either your position or that of other survivors.

▷ HOW TO KILL A ZOMBIE USING A BOW AND ARROW

Virtually anyone can fire off an arrow from a bow, but few can do so accurately enough to hit a zombie in the head at distances of 55 yards (50 m) or more. The bow is a weapon that requires long hours of practice and dedication to master, but with time it can become a powerful and deadly weapon in your anti-zombie arsenal. Always ensure that you carry a supporting melee weapon when you are out with a bow, even if you have support fighters around you.

STEP 1
CONFIRM TARGET

Confirm the target with your dominant eye. You need to assess factors such as distance and wind speed before preparing for your shot. Ensure that you have the right kit including an arm guard and quiver to store your arrows.

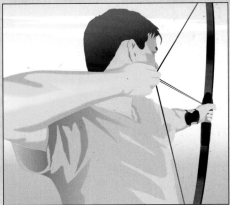

STEP 2
TAKE AIM

Ensure that you are in the correct stance. You should be comfortable but with a firm hand on the weapon and using your back muscles as an anchor point. Use three fingers to pull back the arrow in the split-finger style.

CLASS	PROJECTILE ACTION	RESULT	OUTCOME	ACTION REQUIRED
A FULL HEAD SHOT	Projectile enters through any part of the head.	80% plus of the zombie brain destroyed.	Zombie is out of action.	No follow up action required, just a smug grin.
B GLANCING HEAD SHOT	Projectile hits the head but not centrally.	Less than 80% of the zombie brain destroyed.	Zombie will recoil and may fall under the impact but is still dangerous and mobile.	This zombie will require a further projectile or follow-up with a hand weapon to kill.
C ZOMBIE PINNED	Projectile pierces a bodypart and pins the zombie down.	No damage to the brain.	The zombie struggles to move. If the hit is sufficient, the creature may end up tearing a limb or arm off in its efforts to stagger on.	A pin shot reduces the mobility of a zombie, but further action will be required to dispatch it.
D BODY HIT	Projectile pierces the chest or stomach in comic fashion.	No damage to the brain.	The projectile may or may not impede movement, but the creature is still very much a threat.	This zombie will require a further projectile or to be taken out with a hand weapon.
E COMPLETE MISS	Projectile misses the target.	No damage to the brain. Let's just hope you didn't hit any survivors.	In most cases, zombies will not 'clock' the appearance of projectile weapons. They could well ignore it and continue on.	A degree of embarrassment, followed by hours of rigorous practice with your weapon.

STEP 3
FIRE

Hold the bow arm towards your zombie target and aim down the spine of the arrow. Use a sight if you have one fitted. Release the arrow by relaxing the fingers, ensuring that the action is a as smooth as possible.

STEP 4
ASSESS KILL

Assess your kill using the Ministry of Zombies categorization system above and determine your next action. Where possible, retrieve your arrow when it is safe to do so and remember to always carry a hand weapon for close combat.

IMPROVING ACCURACY

▶ Join your local archery club.
▶ Get the right kit and get expert advice on the right bow for you.
▶ Wear green if you really think it helps.
▶ As you gain experience, you will need to practice against moving targets. This is not something most clubs will offer. One idea is to have a zombie target on wheels and someone to pull it from side to side as you take your shot.

ZOMBIE COMBAT AND WEAPONS

THE CROSSBOW

Over recent years, the crossbow has become the weapon of choice for the many zombie survivalists around the world who have no access to firearms. Global sales from the world's top five manufacturers of modern crossbows have increased 43% and this is attributed at least in part to fears of a zombie apocalypse. Easier to master than a bow, new models are now quick to reload and many are equipped with optical scopes.

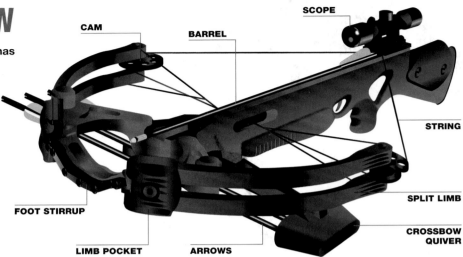

CAM
BARREL
SCOPE
STRING
SPLIT LIMB
CROSSBOW QUIVER
ARROWS
LIMB POCKET
FOOT STIRRUP

▷ THE SILENT KILL – USING A CROSSBOW AGAINST THE DEAD

A modern crossbow will be equipped with a safety catch. A cocked crossbow which is locked will obviously be more ready for use.

Fighters using ranged weapons should always be armed with a secondary melee weapon for hand-to-hand combat.

Always be aware of the wind direction when approaching the dead by stealth. Zombies have a keen sense of smell so stay down wind if possible. The best strategy with a crossbow is to make targeted kills such as taking out a zombie which happens to be blocking your way ahead. It will take time to reload so ensure that any noise you make doesn't attract more of the dead. As with every ranged weapon, get to know how the different weather conditions will affect your shot, particularly the wind and rain. Finally, ensure that you maintain your weapon. This means regular cleaning of the barrel groove in particular and try to gather up your bolts where you can as precision replacements will be very hard to make.

ACCESSORIES

▶ A poncho (not the theme park plastic ones given on water rides), an authentic Mexican chequered one.
▶ A Chopper bike (motorbike not a chopper bicycle).
▶ A shoot-from-the-hip hillbilly attitude.
▶ Optional leather jacket.

STEP 1
CONFIRM TARGET

Creeping through the trees, the fighter is planning on a silent kill to prevent the other creatures around 'clocking' his presence. Pause before firing to help control the breathing. A short rest of a few seconds is advised. Crossbows are very susceptible to any shaking or movement and this will misdirect the bolt.

> **THERE IS NO DOUBT THAT THE CROSSBOW IS NOW SEEN AS THE STANDARD FOR ZOMBIE SURVIVALISTS AND ALL OF OUR SALES FIGURES POINT TO PEOPLE WANTING TO BE PREPARED, WITH A WEAPON THEY CAN REALLY TRUST.**

MIKE ALDERSON, CEO CENTURY WEAPONS LTD

Many modern crossbow bolts will rip right through a brittle zombie skull, tearing chunks of the rotting grey brain matter as it passes through.

However, the zombie-specific ZK-100 bolt is designed with a bulge just after the point so that that once the tip pierces, the bulge follows into the zombie brain, causing far more damage than a regular bolt. It is estimated that a ZK-100 bolt will inflict 61% more brain damage than a standard bolt – that's significantly more zombie-busting power.

OTHER RANGED WEAPONS

A ranged weapon can deal with a zombie from a greater distance as opposed to a melee or hand weapon, which requires close combat. These weapons are a safe way to deal with the dead as you won't come anywhere near the snack radius of the zombies. However, they are, generally speaking, weapons that require more skill to operate and demand much from the user in terms of hours of practice and precision accuracy.

Weapons such as javelins and catapults are also worth investigation but again require a substantial period of training to achieve anything like the level of accuracy required to be effective. There are, however, alternatives that, under the right conditions, can be used to hit the dead from a safe distance. Dropping items such as bricks from a height is remarkably effective if you can get them on target. Where it is safe to do so, survivors under siege may start taking down a non-essential wall and engaging in what is known as 'zombie brick toss'.

STEP 2
FIRE

If it's a difficult shot, aim low and at the chest. Quickly reload, which takes 5–10 seconds for a skilled user, and deliver a second bolt to the head to finish the target. Be aware that the noise of a pin shot may attract more of the walking dead, particularly if the zombie starts groaning and tugging.

STEP 3
ASSESS KILL

Reload and return the safety catch. You are now clear to silently pass your kill. This shot can be very useful if you are escorting a party of foragers etc. Obviously, if you can retrieve the bolt then do so but do not risk a kill confirmation if it is unsafe to do so.

ZOMBIE COMBAT AND WEAPONS

MELEE WEAPONS

Many zombie survivalists view their hand held or melee weapon as the single most important piece of kit they have. It's something that is always within reach and is carried whether they are out on patrol or within a secure 'green zone' perimeter. It's the human ability to use a hand weapon that can really give you the edge in this battle for survival so soak up the knowledge over the next few pages and consider your choices carefully. Some desperate people will face the zombie apocalypse with whatever weapon happens to be around – it could be a rolling pin, a garden tool or even a small branch. However, those

planning to survive a plague of the walking dead have a chance to plan and think things through – to get something with the right weight, something durable and something that is going to save lives when the zombies come knocking.

Few countries have restrictions on melee weapons you can keep around the home but it will no doubt worry most local police forces if you start to purchase large quantities of machetes or swords. It is well-worth going along to your nearest police stations and explaining your zombie concerns – you'll be surprised how many officers are worried about the same thing.

▷ EVERYDAY HAND WEAPONS & LOCATIONS

The typical home is bristling with weapons you can use to defend yourself against both the dead and looters. However, pre-warned is pre-armed, so don't find yourself scrabbling through the kitchen drawer looking for a potato peeler – prepare now! Here are some useful ideas for weapons you can find around most homes. Be creative, once you start looking you'll find weapons everywhere – that heavy wooden tray may be a useful clubbing weapon, maybe you could take one of them out with Granny's wooden leg. Look around with fresh eyes. Do the same thing at the office or school and make a mental list of any potential weapons.

THE CAR

Caught on the road during a zombie crisis? Fear not, your vehicle is the perfect battering ram. Maintain a reasonable speed and go for glancing side blows to the dead rather than clean up and over the hood ramming. As for melee weapons, car doors are perfect whacking weapons.

KEY ITEM

A quality tire iron is a great zombie-bashing tool. There are some drawbacks in terms of length, but in the first desperate hours it will get the job done.

THE GARAGE

Grab a baseball, cricket or any decent sports bat and you'll have a real fighting chance. Forget golf clubs as they tend to bend on first contact. Add nails to give your weapon that extra zip. A well-stocked garage is a veritable treasure trove of weapons against the dead so make sure you're first to the hammer.

KEY ITEM

With perfect balance, a purpose-made handle and smooth action, few melee weapons beat a cricket or baseball bat. You can add nails or barbed wire to 'spice up' your weapon.

PREPARATION FOR THE DESPERATE

If you are reading this and the zombies are slobbering at your window then it's safe to assume you have become a believer. Here's what you should spend the next hours doing:

1 **SECURE YOUR LOCATION** – your first action should be to close and lock all downstairs windows and doors. Once this is done work around the building checking that every opening is secure.

2 **GATHER YOUR SURVIVORS** – get whoever is within the sealed perimeter together. Ensure they understand that the building has been sealed. If anyone wants to leave, manage their exit so that you can seal the doors after them.

3 **WEAPONS** – next priority is to get everyone armed with at least a basic weapon. Once you have your weapons ensure that the building is fully clear of any dead – patrol in pairs if you can.

4 **WATER AND FOOD** – there is a great deal of water trapped in various systems around most buildings so locate any tanks and isolate them. It is a good idea to have another survivor collecting all the food together. Start rationing from the moment you are sealed in.

5 **JUST SURVIVING** – If you have the supplies then convince the rest of your party to stay put for at least the short-term. If you assess your location and it's hopeless then you may need to move but it is far safer to stay where you are if you can. Ensure that you have a guard posted at all times and start to think through your survival plans.

THAT MIGHT GET YOU THROUGH THE FIRST FEW WEEKS OF A MAJOR ZOMBIE OUTBREAK BUT YOU ARE GOING TO HAVE TO LEARN FAST AND TOUGHEN UP IF YOU WANT TO SURVIVE MUCH LONGER!

THE KITCHEN

Forget the knives as these weapons will simply go through the rotting flesh of the dead. Instead, look for any heavy rolling pins or wooden cutting boards to help get you 'cooking' in the zombie-bashing business. As a last resort, you can always throw the microwave or toaster at them.

KEY ITEM

An old fashioned rolling pin is as perfect for zombie bashing as is it for making delicious pastries and treats. Crack a few zombie heads then bake yourself a celebratory pie afterwards – just ensure you wash off any blood first.

THE BEDROOM

Pull a drawer out, empty it and you have a useful one time weapon. Sheets can be used to throw over a zombie, allowing you to make an escape. A zombie attack is also the perfect opportunity to use any bad art you have on the wall as a weapon – it may not do much damage but at least you will be rid of it.

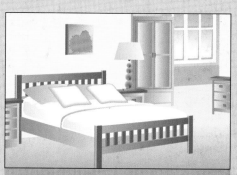

KEY ITEM

A lampshade with a heavy base will make an acceptable emergency club. Always remove the electrical cord to prevent it wrapping around and tripping you. Keep the lampshade if you like the color.

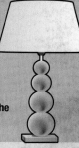

Honor any Celtic heritage by grabbing Grandad's shillelagh from the wall and hoping it isn't just a ceremonial one. Any family swords, shields or daggers could be put to good use ensuring your own survival.

THERE'S NO NEED TO RESORT TO FLINGING YOUR PRECIOUS RECORDS IF OTHER ITEMS ARE AROUND

ZOMBIE COMBAT AND WEAPONS

WEIRD, EXOTIC AND DIY

So far we've covered some of the much-loved classics of zombie combat, from firearms to baseball bats and several cool weapons in-between; however, the zombie apocalypse will also present an opportunity to get creative with your choice of arms. So, if you've always coveted thy neighbor's powerful nail gun then now is the time to get out and buy yourself one. These amazing machines cause around 40,000 injuries around the world every year and so their reputation pretty much speaks for itself. Basically, if you have a weapon which is robust and can do the business on a zombie brain then why not innovate to use something you've designed for yourself – be it a gun firing six inch nails or specially adapted chainsaw with cool skull and cross bone markings. There are so many options out there including sledgehammers and machetes, you are really spoilt for choice.

There is also a wide range of weapons available on the internet, some of which have been designed with zombie busting in mind, such as the lead 'zombie-crusher' baseball bat from the Hero Sports Group.

THE 'WOULD-BE NINJA'

A survey completed by *Car and Gun Magazine* in the US in 2006 asked readers to recommend the ideal ranged weapon with which to fight zombies. The top answer was quite rightly the crossbow, but more than 31% of respondents reported that they had not only ordered but also practiced with ninja-throwing stars in preparation for the zombie apocalypse.

WHY THROWING STARS WILL GET YOU KILLED:

▶ The chances are you are not a trained ninja and the likelihood of you hitting a zombie head with a throwing star is very slim.
▶ Even if you do hit the creature, a star will not penetrate deep enough to do any serious damage.
▶ Wearing your black pyjama outfit will look very conspicuous as you slink through the abandoned streets. You may also sweat a lot, attracting even more of the dead.

▷ FIRE AND THE DEAD

As a rule, zombies and fire don't mix. For most desiccated ghouls, even the hint of a flame seems to halt their advance. However, this rule is by no means universal. For example, starting a fire at an encampment is a great way to attract the dead – it seems that the movement or scent of the smoke just attracts them.

There are literally hundreds of ways you can attack the walking dead with fire – just remember that a burning zombie may still lumber forward. The heat of the flame needs to destroy at least 80% of the brain to take the creature down. Burn times on a classic zombie are typically 1-3 minutes – this is from the moment its head is alight to the moment it collapses. This timeframe will depend on factors such as climate and the clothing the zombie is wearing. It often surprises inexperienced zombie fighters that when they throw a petrol bomb or set a zombie on fire, the creature will frequently keep shuffling towards them, even as it is blazing away. Such creatures are called 'flamers' and you generally get flamers when the fire is on the body of the zombie rather than the head.

PETROL BOMBS

Petrol Bombs, or Molotov Cocktails, can be made easily using any flammable liquid. They are then best hurled into packs of the dead. In Ministry of Zombies tests, even larger petrol bombs did little real damage to a group of zombies. A good hit may take out one or two but they are not as effective as untrained survivors believe. Beware of the odd flaming zombie running towards your site – they have a nasty habit of spreading fires.

COMBAT AND WEAPONS
THE CLASSIC CHAINSAW

CLOSE COMBAT? NO NEED FOR QUIET?

Then embark on a death-defying slashing fest, which can hack tens of zombies into casserole chunks. That's what the mighty chainsaw offers – a powerful handheld weapon with a reputation for carnage amongst zombie fighters.

COMBAT TECHNIQUES

Combat techniques against the dead when using a chainsaw used to be based on aggressive slashing, but improvements in chainsaw technology – in particular lighter machines – have allowed a more skilful combat art to develop. Known as the 'Dance of the Chainsaw', it leans surprisingly on ballet, focusing on balance and poise when in combat. The fighter launches a series of different moves to counter any lunge made by a zombie and then returns to a well-balanced 'aplomb' position.

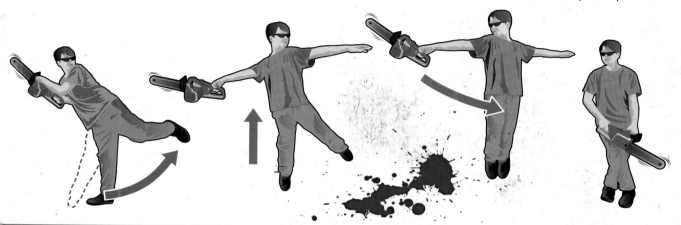

FLAMETHROWER

If you have one handy, the flamethrower can be a devastating weapon against the dead. Always remember to accompany each flamethrower-armed survivor with other fighters to offer protection and fire using short, controlled bursts. This weapon can be particularly useful for clearing long corridors of the dead. Always allow a few minutes for the ghouls to properly cook.

CITY OF THE DEAD FIRES

As your group starts to liberate more territory from the dead, you will doubtless come across some towns or cities which are so dangerously infested with the dead that it's easy to take out the whole site, then go building-to-building zombie clearing. It is good practice to send a vehicle with a loud speaker through the area first to warn survivors and give them time to evacuate.

ZOMBIE COMBAT AND WEAPONS

COMBAT FOR THE ELDERLY

A zombie apocalypse will be a particularly hard time for the elderly for, although they have much wisdom and many interesting stories to share, particularly about the 'good old days', few are ready to defend themselves against the walking dead. Well, that's what many think. However, UK and American charity organisation Age Zombie Awareness (AZA) has been working for over a decade and in nations across the world to prepare the elderly for a zombie outbreak. In fact, to date almost 100,000 people over the age of 65 in Europe and North America have been through basic zombie combat training, making them one of the best prepared demographic groups. The AZA training includes support with developing Bug-Out plans and food storage advice as well as actual combat training and top tips for playing bingo. The Ministry of Zombies is the AZA's only licensed partner and the following content was designed by their experts and is part of their most popular course 'Senior Citizen, Senior Survivor'.

'DANCE LIKE FRED ASTAIRE AND STING LIKE MUHAMMAD ALI!' – A FIGHTING MOTTO FROM THE AZA TRAINING COURSE

▷ WALKING FRAME DEFENSE TECHNIQUES FROM THE AZA COURSE

STEP 1
THE VALUE OF A HEARING AID

After a foraging mission to the shops, an elderly survivor is targeted by a shuffling zombie. The creature approaches its target. Our survivor easily picks up the noise of its dragging feet by wearing an enhanced and highly sensitive hearing aid. She does not respond immediately as she is also wearing a ghoulish perfume musk which may make the zombie ignore her. No luck this time as the zombie continues to approach. She braces for action.

STEP 2
THE FOUR-PRONGED LOCK

The survivor only springs into action once the creature is within range. Once it is within a a few feet she swings her walking frame up and traps the zombie, blocking its approach. If there is a wall or fence nearby, she can pin the zombie against it. Either way, the ghoul is contained as she either calls for help or makes plans for her escape.

COMBAT WITH A WALKING STICK

The course 'Senior Citizen, Senior Survivor' includes sessions on zombie combat using everyday objects such as shopping bags, a rolled-up newspaper and even a bulky TV guide. However, a particular emphasis is placed on training for combat using a walking stick. The AZA has developed a range of walking sticks which have been adapted to include a shooting spike at the end. This spike can be released at the touch of a button on the handle and can be used to pin a zombie and keep the creature at a safe distance. Target practice sessions encourage elderly combatants to first aim for the chest before honing their skills with an accurate head shot. A jab to the head followed with a spring-loaded spike jab will dispatch most zombies.

GUNS FOR GRANNY

The organization Age Zombie Awareness does not currently deliver a course on firearms for the elderly, but it does highlight in several pamphlets that many older people, particularly veterans of the Second World War and other conflicts, are already trained and experienced with various types of gun. In fact, pioneering work has already been completed by a group of these veterans to create a zombie-busting gun particularly for the elderly. It is based on the antique 'blunderbuss' used by an elderly Irish grandmother in Belfast in 1979. Other survivors were amused as Mrs Cassidy took aim at a group of approaching zombies but were stunned when the shot from her brass musket spread and destroyed every one of the dead. Mrs Cassidy herself had her wheeled shopping basket specially adapted to carry the weapon and additional iron pellets.

STEP 3
THE FRAME FLICK

With no other survivors in the area and more of the dead nearby, our elderly survivor does not want to call for help so she uses all of her strength to pull the walking frame back and then flick it sideways, sending the creature tumbling to the ground. She can then either deliver a walking frame stamp, which will impale one of the struts through the soft, brittle skull of the zombie, or just make her escape.

ZOMBIE COMBAT AND WEAPONS

FIXED DEFENSES

What could be better than sitting in a deckchair behind your defenses hearing the pleasing snap as another zombie is caught in that mantrap you 'foraged' from the museum, or the moan as another ghoul tumbles into one of your spiked pits? Well, taking out zombies requires more focus than this.

Whether you are defending a major settlement of survivors or just going it alone in your gun shop, fixed defenses can help deal with the zombies while you watch with an insane grin.

For the first weeks of a major zombie outbreak, the streets will be chaos with desperate and unprepared survivors running everywhere in search of safety. This is not the time to be leaving your carefully prepared stronghold. Stay inside during this period and 'run silent'. However, as you reach the one-month point, things will be quieter and you should consider working out some viable fixed defenses to improve your set-up. For example, are there any large vehicles nearby you can use to block off roads, or ways you could extend a fence to create an additional perimeter.

Make use of any natural barriers such as rivers and don't overlook the obvious such as sealing or bricking up a house to create a large defensive barrier. You may not have the resources to dig a moat around your property so make use of what's around you to create significant zombie barriers, then augment your perimeter with some cunning traps to ensnare the walking dead.

▶ SUNKEN DEFENSES

SUNKEN DEFENSE 1
THE DITCH OR HOLE

The simple ditch or any hole is an obstacle to the walking dead as they frequently lack the foresight to avoid it and the dexterity to get out. If you lack the resources for a full 6-foot (2 m) ditch around your home, try lifting the man-hole covers and howl with laughter as the dead tumble in. Just ensure that you don't follow them and that there are no survivors sheltering down there.

SUNKEN DEFENSE 2
THE GHOUL PIT

This is basically any hole or ditch which has been filled with obstructions to do damage to the dead. The idea is that as the zombies fall in, they are impaled on the spikes and can be dealt with at your leisure. Again, always ensure that you place a warning above such a trap. Zombies can't read so you don't need to worry about them dodging your carefully-prepared traps.

SUNKEN DEFENSE 3
THE MOAT

The last of the sunken defenses. Unless you live in a 15th-century chateau, it is unlikely that your home will be surrounded by a moat. However, sensible use of a flooded ditch or river can be a useful way of securing a flank from zombie attack. Of course, the dead could always float over, but it does at least give some defense. Do not start digging a moat around your home unless you have the room and planning permission.

ZOMBIE COMBAT AND WEAPONS
MAN (ZOMBIE) TRAPS

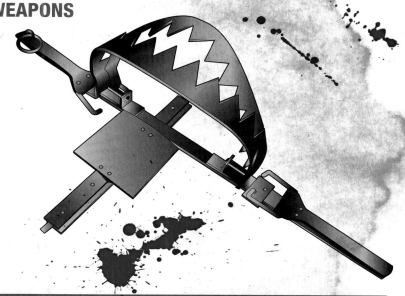

Both the modern claymore anti-personnel mine and iron man trap are designed to wound rather than kill humans so their effect on the dead is marginal. For example, the man trap was used by landowners to fend off poachers and was banned in virtually every country. The serrated edges of the metal jaws can cut right through zombie limbs and inflict horrific wounds, but are not designed to kill. The claymore anti-personnel mine fires hundreds of ball bearings into the air but presents no particular threat to a zombie. An effective zombie trap must delay, kill or incapacitate a significant number of the dead to be useful. Targeted killing is no use.

▷ SPIKED DEFENSES

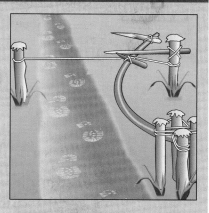

SPIKED DEFENSE 1
DEFENSIVE ARRAY

Low-tech solutions work on the dead and any spiked defenses are ideal for slowing the dead down. Zombies are clumsy and will always catch themselves on any spikes or wires. Even a chord stretched across the road could cause them to stumble. Be sure to hang some form of warning on your defenses. A makeshift barrier won't be a watertight perimeter and beware of any holes through which crawlers could creep.

SPIKED DEFENSE 2
RAZOR WIRE

Again, this is designed to slow zombies down as they become entangled in razor or barb wire. It can be very useful where laid in multiple layers. A horde of the walking dead will get through such a barrier eventually, but it can serve as a useful delaying tactic. If you don't have access to the real thing, any DIY store will have chicken wire or mesh which, with the addition of a few cuts and jagged edges, can be a worthy substitute.

SPIKED DEFENSE 3
TRIGGER WIRE

There are literally thousands of variations of the trigger-wire trap you can use to create effective anti-zombie fortifications. Most are spring-loaded and designed to make noise as well as take out the zombie unfortunate enough to trip them. Smaller trigger-wire traps can be used to catch small mammals such as rabbits and therefore provide a useful supplement of fresh meat.

ZOMBIE COMBAT AND WEAPONS

ZOMBIE PROFILES ——

Something that confuses most fighters when they first encounter the walking dead is the obvious variation. To the untrained eye it appears that there are different kinds of zombie, that the zombic condition somehow creates different symptoms in some humans and there is some truth in this. In zombiology, we call these zombie 'types' as they are in no way variations in any medical definition. They are all humans who have been transformed into ravenous walking corpses by the zombie virus. However, with factors such as climate, injury, age profile and even look, the zombie fighter can find themselves facing a variety of these different zombie types.

The Ministry of Zombies recognizes seven official types of zombie although there are considerable variations and some types may be combined. Know these types, their attack vectors and how to fight them.

INFECTED HUMANS

Some zombie fighters recognize an eighth zombie type, infected humans, as although they may not have yet developed the symptoms of the zombic condition, they are still a clear danger to any living survivor. Typically these individuals know they've been infected but will do anything in their power to hide this fact from fellow survivors. Ironically, they seem drawn to survivor groups and in the short time they have left, will try to work their way into a group.

If you encounter any stray survivors you suspect of being infected you can either take them in and then keep them in a secure compound under observation for 48 hours or tell them to be on their way if you are short on supplies or suspect their motives. If you choose the latter, use the following advice:

1. Give a clear warning **'Stay back or I will use lethal force'**. Do not allow them to approach even if they insist they just want to talk. You can always throw out food and supplies if they need it.

2. Depending on the situation, you may fire a warning shot. Do not allow this individual to join your group if they have clear bite marks. If you are not going to quarantine them then they need to be either on their way or you will need to take them down.

3. Keep watching if they choose to walk away. Be wary in case they try to sneak back towards you. This is something virtually every infected survivor will do. They may hide and wait until night before trying to get into your compound. It is a sad fact that few infected humans will walk away from a human settlement.

▶ CLASSIC ZOMBIE

KEY FEATURES

▶ Will display classic zombie signs such as pale grey-blue skin color.
▶ Can appear 'human-like' with no visible wound.
▶ Others will be in terrible condition, with dry open wounds or unsightly mold patches.

ATTACK VECTOR

▶ Will stagger or 'run' at some pace towards any living human.
▶ Arms will be reaching forward to grab.
▶ Danger of infected scratch.
▶ Main objective is to cram flesh into mouth.
▶ The neck and forearm are the most common bite targets.

COMBAT STRATEGY

1. Identify the zombie (use picture if unsure). This will be an important step early on as trigger-happy survivors open fire on everything and everyone.
2. A heavy blow or shot to the head will do the business – aiming to destroy at least 80% of the brain.
3. Confirm the kill with a foot stamp or club hit. Always check your zombie kills before notching them up on your zombie kill chart.

ALL ZOMBIE TYPES ARE DANGEROUS, ALL CAN KILL BUT SOME ARE MORE DEADLY THAN OTHERS

▶ BLOATERS

KEY FEATURES

- ▶ Bulky and over-sized zombies, bloated by the build-up of acid and gas within the corpse.
- ▶ Humid and tropical conditions mean that this excess liquid builds pressure within the zombie, particularly in the stomach and intestines.
- ▶ Bloaters can be very dangerous in confined spaces and are prone to block entire corridors.

ATTACK VECTOR

- ▶ A bloater has the same flesh-feeding instinct as any other zombie.
- ▶ Its bulk makes it a slow opponent and an easy target.
- ▶ It stumbles towards targets.
- ▶ If it trips, it can suffocate opponents in folds of putrid and rotting flesh.
- ▶ It is prone to necromesis – the ejecting of stomach acid and bile at velocity.
- ▶ In confined spaces, bloaters will use their lumbering bulk to block escape routes.

COMBAT STRATEGY

1. Never shoot or pierce a bloater at close range. These creatures are full of pressurized bile and infected vomit. They will explode if punctured.
2. Create distance between yourself and a bloater with a strong two handed shove. Alternatively, a double drop kick when it is safe to do so.
3. After creating aforementioned distance (you need at least 10 feet, or 3 meters), aim a shot, arrow or spear towards the head of the creature. If you can leave the body then do, but if you need to deflate it then a long hollow pole shoved into the side of the creature will allow the pressure to be released safely.

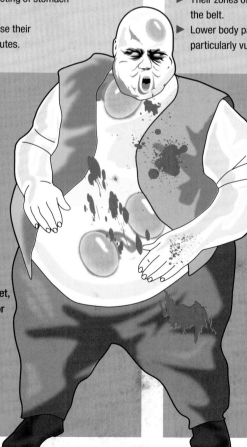

▶ KIDDIE GHOULS

KEY FEATURES

- ▶ Children are infected with the zombie virus in the same way as adults.
- ▶ The conversion process is slightly faster in children under 16.
- ▶ Kiddie ghouls tend to be faster and more dextrous than the adult zombie due to their growing muscle mass.

ATTACK VECTOR

- ▶ The right kiddie ghoul can reduce even the most seasoned zombie fighter to inaction.
- ▶ These creatures use that second of uncertainty to race forward at pace.
- ▶ Their zones of attack are all below the belt.
- ▶ Lower body parts are therefore particularly vulnerable.

COMBAT STRATEGY

1. Be prepared for the harrowing sight of a ten-year-old zombie. It's tragic, but never forget they are the undead and should be destroyed in the same way as adult zombies.
2. Be cautious of kicking these tiny terrors. Even experienced fighters are prone to miss these fast moving creatures, allowing them to sink their teeth into the flesh or kneecap of the defender.
3. If you are armed, take your time as you will typically only get one shot and remember, when under stress shoot low. The idea is to stop the creature.
4. If you are unarmed then time your kick as the creature is just about to reach you. Aim it towards the chest to avoid it being knocked over by your kick and into your body.

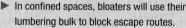

ZOMBIE COMBAT AND WEAPONS

▶ LIMBLESS WONDERS

KEY FEATURES

▶ A zombie that has been through some trauma and has its arms severed.

▶ Limbless wonders tend to be quicker than full-bodied zombies due to their reduced body weight.

▶ They have fewer attack options than other zombies, with no grabbing hands.

ATTACK VECTOR

▶ Limbless wonders will run straight at you.

▶ They tend to dash at almost human-like speed.

▶ Their only objective is to rush forward and bury their jaws into your flesh.

▶ They often tilt their head down in a headbutt maneuver before their final attack.

▶ Where a creature's limbs have been severed below the elbow, be cautious as the stumps tend to be sharp and jagged, making them very effective slashing weapons in combat.

COMBAT STRATEGY

1. When armed these creatures are easily dealt with, but when unarmed and caught unaware by a limbless wonder, always secure your balance first. If the creature is very close, you can risk a quick dodge with your foot left out and the attacking zombie will trip and be sent crashing to the floor.

2. A powerful jumping kick or two-handed shove to the zombie's chest will unbalance it and send it the floor.

3. Follow up with a trusty stamp to the head. Generally, once they are on the ground, limbless wonders struggle to get up.

▶ CRAWLERS

KEY FEATURES

▶ Zombies with both legs missing are known as crawlers.

▶ These creatures tend to be very degraded due to their ground-hugging 'lifestyle'.

▶ Crawlers are a particularly harrowing sight and may have entrails such as intestines dragging behind them.

ATTACK VECTOR

▶ Crawlers move by dragging themselves along the ground with their jagged fingers.

▶ They can squeeze through the smallest holes in fences or gates and are prone to surprise the unprepared.

▶ They are mostly noiseless as they lay horizontal and typically attack the lower leg.

COMBAT STRATEGY

1. Sensible footwear should be worn. High boots will offer some protection from the grab or bite of an unseen crawler.

2. Where a crawler is visible, they can be easily dealt with most safely by impaling them with a long spear. This way you don't need to go close to the creature.

3. Where you are surprised by a crawler, leap into the air as soon as you notice it and aim to come down squarely with both feet, in what is known as a 'superstamp', to cave in the skull of the crawler. Do not attempt this maneuver in flip-flops. Sensible footwear is advisable whenever you face zombies in combat.

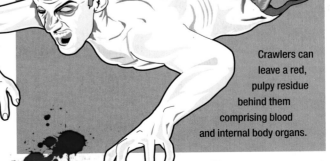

Crawlers can leave a red, pulpy residue behind them comprising blood and internal body organs.

SEVERED HEADS

KEY FEATURES

▶ Zombie heads can survive when severed from the body for weeks.

▶ Zombiology does not yet understand how these isolated heads 'live'.

▶ The zombie has very little movement, but it has been known to move by wriggling its jaws along the ground.

ATTACK VECTOR

▶ Severed zombie heads have only one vector of attack.

▶ They will try to take a bite out of any foot or leg that comes close enough.

▶ They are capable of reaching forward a few inches but no more.

▶ Where they become trapped in trees or on shelves, they can drop onto the unwary, taking a chunk of flesh as they fall.

COMBAT STRATEGY

1 If you find a zombie head in the open then take the chance to improve the morale of your group by trying to deal with it creatively. Firstly, approach the head with good balance and a firm footing.

2 Swing leg with force and make sure you get a good connection with the soccer ball-sized head.

3 Scream goal as you run back to your group, waving your hands in the air or perhaps removing a garment and swinging it around your head wildly. Be sure that you are not kicking any severed head zombie or 'snapper' into another group of humans.

Alternatively, you could just stick a knife into the top of the skull to deal with a stray head. Always be careful to stay out of snapping range so ensure that you use a long blade. Don't go trying it with a pen knife as you will need to bury it deep within the brain to do the job.

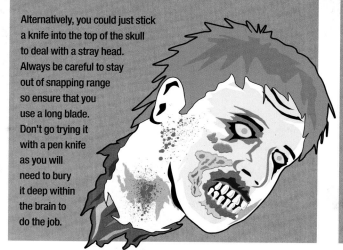

ATTRACTIVE ZOMBIES

KEY FEATURES

▶ Some zombies can appear almost 'attractive' to living survivors.

▶ The world of the celebrity will be hit hard by the zombie virus.

▶ Survivors may be confused or distracted when coming face to face with one of these attractive-but-deadly creatures.

ATTACK VECTOR

▶ An attractive zombie will attack, the same as any other ghoul.

▶ It may 'learn' something of the distracting effect it has on survivors and use this as a hunting technique.

▶ Expect prolonged eye-to-eye contact before teeth-to-flesh munching activity begins.

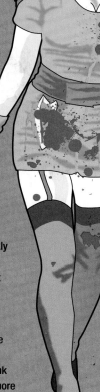

COMBAT STRATEGY

1 If you encounter any of our beloved reality TV stars – open fire. Forget the 'identify as a zombie' or warning stage – just fire. Chances are they are zombies.

2 Avoid eye contact with these beguiling creatures. They have no supernatural power, but they can draw you in.

3 Blast the creature as quickly as possible. A direct head shot with a shotgun is best to destroy any lingering good looks.

Some fighters insist that female zombies use the long, lingering stare more whereas moody, lank hair male zombies, attempt a more brooding look.

OUT AND ABOUT IN ZOMBIE TOWN

Whether you're foraging in a nearby house for supplies or relocating to a safer long-term location, there will be many occasions during the zombie apocalypse when you need to leave your fortified home and head out into zombie town.

Make no mistake, any transport in 'bandit country' will be dangerous and any human movement will attract the attention of the dead. If you are well prepared and have your full 90-day supplies sorted and stored then you shouldn't need to venture outside of your secure base for weeks. However, it's still a good idea to have a quick scout around on about Day 50 to survey your immediate area. Start by observing from a high vantage point such as a loft window, then check out some nearby homes. If you are in an area of low zombie density, use this as a chance to stock up on any supplies you find and join up with other survivors. During your initial forays into zombie town, travel light and stay close to your home base. By Day 70, you should have completed a serious assessment of your current location and immediate area. It's then time to decide whether you move on or develop a settlement where you are.

THE ZOMBIE TRAVEL SAFETY CODE

Regardless of how you are travelling, learn the Zombie Travel Safety Code and always consider it before you travel. This code was developed by the US government in the 1980s but was never used due to concerns over public opinion. They even went as far as designing a Zombie Safety character known as the 'Zombie Safety Chameleon' which was meant to educate people about zombie safety and 'staying hidden' from the dead. Many of the key points are instinctive to experienced zombie fighters. For example, staying silent when moving and first contact protocols. However, the code has gone on to form the basis of virtually all zombie survival training. It is important that you maintain a good level of alertness when out foraging or on patrol in zombie town and it is recommended that you are never more than three hours away from a secure base. As a final pointer, be careful to avoid picking up a straggler – that is a shambling zombie who picks up your scent and staggers after you but can't catch up.

OUT AND ABOUT IN ZOMBIE TOWN
FORAGING – IS IT STEALING?

Your 90-day survival plan is designed to give you a fighting chance in the zombie apocalypse. It hopefully means you won't need to go out desperately searching for a tin of peaches and ironically getting yourself eaten looking for something to eat.

In 2009, and promoted by a series of natural disasters, the United Nations in New York issued the following clarification on emergency foraging in disaster areas:

▶ Survivors may make reasonable use of the resources around them providing they are neither in use nor claimed by another survivor.
▶ Survivors may not hoard excessive quantities of food, water or resources and may not profiteer from their collection.
▶ Any weapons of mass destruction are excluded from this declaration.

Basically, as long as the property is clearly abandoned and there are no other survivors there, it's 'help yourself'.

ON ANY FORAGING MISSION make a list of what you are after and don't be tempted to overload with stock you don't need. Target the essentials first and work to keep your 90-day stock topped up. If you encounter armed survivors who claim the supplies as their own, back away as there should be plenty for everyone in the first year of the zombie apocalypse. It is best to avoid the well-known locations in the first months of the crisis. Supermarkets, gun shops and shopping centers will become the focus for various unsavory gangs of looters and thieves. The best scenario is if you can find one of those large white supermarket warehouses that tend to sit on the edge of town. Many of these buildings look like any other warehouse but inside you'll find enough food and supplies to feed a small army for years. If you manage to secure one of these locations, it may be worth considering it as a long-term settlement location rather than trying to move all of the stocks.

NEVER LEAD A ZOMBIE BACK TO YOUR HOME BASE OR YOU RISK ATTRACTING MORE OF THE WALKING DEAD

STEP 1
EXIT

Always check the coast is clear before exiting a door or your vehicle. A quick scan will normally suffice and don't forget to look behind you. Use hand signals to communicate with fellow survivors and keep noise to a minimum.

STEP 2
BE READY

It's basic: have a version of your Bug-Out Bag and a weapon, and know where your safe locations are. It does mean you won't be able to carry as many supplies when foraging but safety first! Remember that a balanced Bug-Out Bag will be your only lifeline.

STEP 3
SCANNING

Keep your eyes regularly scanning the environment – never stare too long at one building or site. Zombies can be surprisingly quiet so maintain that 360-degree scan every few minutes. When out walking on patrol, always conduct a 360-degree sweep every 65 feet (20 m).

STEP 4
LANDSCAPE

Know your enemy, always look for hidden corners where they are likely to lurk. Clock alternative routes and take in as much about the surrounding area as possible. Be cautious, get to know the area well and stay alive.

STEP 5
FIRST CONTACT

Hide, take out or run – these are options that you need to quickly weigh up. If there is just one zombie, maybe it can be dealt with quietly. If there is a small horde, maybe it is time to retreat coolly out of danger.

STEP 6
AWARENESS

Don't allow your guard to drop for a second. This makes time outside the settlement tiring so ensure you make best use of it and stay somewhere safe overnight. Experienced fighters call this 'staying frosty'.

OUT AND ABOUT IN ZOMBIE TOWN

WALKING IN A WORLD OF THE DEAD

Travelling long distances on foot will be the norm in a world dominated by zombies. Sure, it would be safer going by car, but with blocked roads, burnt-out buildings and collapsed bridges in many cases travel by foot will be the only way. Even when you can use a vehicle, there will be times when you need to leave it to forage within a building or to reach a trapped survivor elsewhere. Your fitness regime will help ensure you have the fortitude for long walks, but here are some guidelines to help you prepare for the pleasures of walking in zombie town. In terms of preparation, start with long walks as part of your training and try to complete at least one 6 to 8-mile (10 to 13-km) walk on top of your normal physical training.

Just remember that you will only move as fast as your slowest survivor. So, if you have the elderly or people overloaded with supplies, you will not only be slower, you may also lose the dynamic ability to respond to zombie attacks. Our main advantage over the dead is our speed and agility – don't negate these or you risk getting eaten.

FEEL THE NEED FOR SPEED?

Assuming you don't have access to a car or that the roads are so choked that you can't get anywhere, there are still some alternatives to travelling on foot but you should always take into account that high speed travel and zombies don't mix well! Here are a few modes you may want to consider:

▶ **BICYCLES** – a decent mountain bike could be a great way to get around once the zombies arrive. You can add panniers to carry supplies in and you would easily be able to out run any zombies.

▶ **ROLLER SKATES** – are you insane? Unless you are a skilful skater – the type that parades around the park in a crop top during summer doing sweeping spins, be very cautious of donning your leotard and skates because of the sheer lack of control.

▶ **MOTORCYCLES** – now we are talking – just imagine surviving the end of the world on a cool chopper bike with your weapons strapped on your back. An all-terrain motorbike would be required not just a street racer.

▶ MRS WOODFORD'S ZOMBIE GUIDE TO DOGS

Legendry British canine expert, Mrs Victoria Woodford, created the following guide in the 1970s to help you prepare your beloved pet for the zombie apocalypse. At the time, little was known about the virus but Mrs Woodford knew the value of a loyal companion and quickly realized that our furry friends may be of great service when the dead rise.

STEP 1
TRAINING TO SMELL

Train your dog to smell zombies by finding a rotting body part and make the dog familiar with the smell. Do not be alarmed if the animal nibbles it, they will not develop the zombic condition.

STEP 2
SMELLING THE DEAD

Now hide a dead zombie and see if the dog can find it. Use short phrases such as 'where's the zombie boy?' to alert the dog that they must scan for the telltale scent of a walking corpse.

CORRECT FOOTWEAR

Believe it or not, a good pair of broken-in walking boots could save your life. If you start to slow down with blisters then you will become a target for any dead in the area.

TRAINING IS IMPORTANT

You should be able to complete up to a five-hour trek per day and be able to sustain this for up to five days. This is a general guide but should be your target in your fitness training.

EARLY STARTS

Try to get started as soon as there is daylight. Darkness is not your friend as zombies have an excellent sense of smell and the lack of light will make your walking route more dangerous.

SNACK RADIUS

Be aware of your snack radius at all times. Keep to the middle of roads where you can and away from blind corners or trees. This can help minimize the risk of a zombie clawing out from nowhere.

EYES AROUND

Every few minutes or so, carry out a slow turn as you walk to scan 360 degrees to check whether there are any zombies who may be stumbling after you. This is a well-known military patrol technique.

ALWAYS BE ARMED

Never be without your weapon. Trekking poles have proved to be very poor when it comes to bashing zombies as many are now made of light fiberglass.

BUG-OUT BAG

Carry a scaled down version of your Bug-Out Bag, even if you are just out foraging. Be equipped with the essentials you need to survive for 24–48 hours away from your main site.

RUN AND HIDE

If you are cornered or become trapped while out walking, find a safe place to hold up and remain silent. If necessary, this could involve you being silent for up to 48 hours so take a book in your pack.

THE RIGHT PACING

The average zombie will not be able to keep up at only a brisk walk and it will conserve your energy. If you exhaust yourself, the dead will just keep coming and you could be overwhelmed.

STEP 3
WALKIES FOR THE DEAD

Experiment with some brisk walks in areas where you know there are rotting corpses. Ensure that you pass within yards of the rotting bodies and allow your canine to pick up the scent and alert you to their presence.

STEP 4
OUT AND ABOUT

Now when the zombies arrive you will be ready. Remember to carry a firearm and continue to congratulate your dog on each 'spot' they make. Be aware that in areas covered with the dead, the strong scent may confuse your dog.

Canines are by far the best pets to train for anti-zombie work and it is rumored that the Chinese Red Army makes extensive use of specially bred Chow Chow dogs to support their anti-zombie patrols. These dogs are not used to attack the dead, simply to alert their human partners that the undead are near. To date, only dogs have proved capable of anti-zombie activity although there is some interesting work being done in Northern England with ferrets.

OUT AND ABOUT IN ZOMBIE TOWN

FIRST-CONTACT PROTOCOLS

After the initial carnage of the zombie apocalypse and as you move outside for the first time, you and your fellow survivors must have a clear set of protocols for dealing with the various individuals and groups you will encounter, including other survivors, zombies and even wild animals. Remember, society will have changed – you will need to change your mind set to match a new and much harsher reality.

INDIVIDUALS AND SMALL GROUPS

The golden rule of the zombie wasteland is to never trust anyone. Sounds harsh but the various scavengers and bandits you meet as you forage for supplies will be desperate and you shouldn't take any chances. Be polite and clear where you can but always back it up with force. Never appear vulnerable and be wary of any tricks designed to make you drop your guard. Basically, you should treat any individual or small group you encounter with caution. In the early days, things can be more informal but as your survivor group grows you will need to adopt strict policies to integrate any new people into your group.

LARGER GROUPS

Here are some first-contact protocols for dealing with any new group of survivors.

1. Always try to 'encounter' groups away from your main site. This will be mean scouting and search patrols. Better to assess them at a neutral location than at your own front door.
2. On first contact, be firm and steady; carefully assess the group's capabilities and intent. Most will be scared, embattled families just looking to survive.
3. It may be an idea to create a meeting point at a prominent location away from the main base. You can daub giant signs or mark the roads with spray paint. You can then hide and observe survivors as they gather at your collection point.
4. No matter how meagre your resources, all new survivors must go through the three stages of entry into the settlement. These are clearing, induction and integration.
5. Some groups will leave you no alternative but to fight. They will seek out your secure location and even assault it. Be ready for human opponents as well as dead ones and ensure that the whole team is ready to defend what you have. These groups will prey on the weak so hopefully overt displays of strength will deter them.

ZOMBIE HORDES

Where you come across a single zombie, it is always best to deal with them silently if possible. Avoid using firearms if you can as any noise will attract more of the walking dead. If you encounter a much larger group, known to survivalists as a 'horde' – then stop and move away as quietly as you can. Do not make any sudden dashes and keep your team in order. Be aware of wind direction as this may carry your scent. Never start a fight without very careful planning as you may find yourself facing more piling out from every side road or alley way.

WILD ANIMALS

Many beloved household pets will be left to fend for themselves in the aftermath of a major zombie outbreak. Now, you don't need to worry about roving gangs of hamsters but feral dogs will become more of a problem as time goes on. If you encounter a pack, never turn your back on it and slowly back away. Keep your weapon ready and if possible have some doggie treats in your kit bag which you can scatter liberally as you withdraw.

DEALING WITH THE CRAZIES

Weirdness will become the norm amongst the desperate and lonely survivors of the wasteland and for some; it will all be too much. Here are some basic guidelines for dealing with those who are rather rudely known as 'The Crazies':

▶ If you or any of your survivor group encounters a 24-carat mental case then the safest principle is to avoid where possible. You may encounter them briefly for the first time, keep any exchange to a minimum and from then on avoid 'mad town'.

▶ Where a crazy just sits watching you from a window or vantage point, avoid eye contact if you can. Do not look at them closely. They may just see you as potential raiders so move on and leave them in peace.

▶ If a crazy runs out in front of you and starts screaming about little people or any other such thing, you must remain calm. Use quiet and understanding language but keep one hand on your weapon. If possible, look for an opportunity to move on and leave the individual.

▶ Remember, the zombie apocalypse will put enormous pressure on people so don't blame them for cracking up. Where you can, you should try to support those in need. Time is a great healer – maybe they will change their 'crazy' ways and they might join your survivor group. You never know.

> DISGUISING YOURSELF AS A ZOMBIE

It is a common myth among many zombie survivalists that you can 'fool' zombies into ignoring you for an extended period by 'dressing up as a zombie'. This tactic has been successful in tests for very short periods of time, but the moment the survivor starts to sweat or gets too close to one of the dead, the zombie will 'clock' the human. It is a dangerous tactic to use but one which can be relied upon for a few minutes of respite in an emergency.

> FEW PEOPLE LIKE BEING COVERED IN ROTTING HUMAN BODY PARTS. IF YOU FIND YOU ARE STARTING TO ENJOY THE EXPERIENCE THEN STOP DOING IT, OR PREPARE TO JOIN THE CRAZY CREW '

▶ Emit a low moan or growl but don't overdo it – this isn't drama school. It doesn't need to be continuous, get a feel for the vibe in your zombie group. If they are silent, you stay silent.

▶ Adopt a tired vacant 'student' look, with your head tilted to one side. Wearing a hooded top covered in blood can really add to the whole effect.

▶ Hang body parts such as intestines around your waist as a belt. Accessorise with other random internal organs in pockets. Ensure that all body parts are rotting.

▶ Wear a torn check shirt and ensure that it is covered in dried blood or at least red paint. Try to keep all flesh covered.

▶ Attempt a shuffling walk, possibly dragging one foot behind you. Again, don't overdo it and avoid the temptation to go faster than the rest of the horde.

▶ Keep your hair greasy and caked in mud or dirt. Add make up to really get that 'corpse look'.

▶ Drag a weapon along in your hand – it is important that you stay armed at all times. Zombies can often be seen dragging items so practice to make it look authentic.

▶ Avoid any close contact with the walking dead – even brushing alongside one of them could give you away if they catch the scent of a fresh human.

▶ Wear lots of deodorant if the weather is hot to help mask the scent of any sweating. And do not try to use this disguise if there is a chance of rain!

▶ Finally, avoid any other humans. It would be one hell of a way to go to survive the zombie apocalypse only to be killed by a fellow survivor who mistook you for a walking corpse!

OUT AND ABOUT IN ZOMBIE TOWN

DRIVING IN ZOMBIE TOWN

Most survivors will have access to a motor vehicle of some sort, be it a fully-equipped, post-apocalyptic-ready Hummer or simply a motorized scooter. You should allow at least four to eight weeks before venturing far from your primary survival site. This will give time for the initial chaos to die down. However, even then, driving in a post-apocalyptic landscape will be fraught with danger and unseen hazards, and that's not even counting the flesh munchers lurking round every corner.

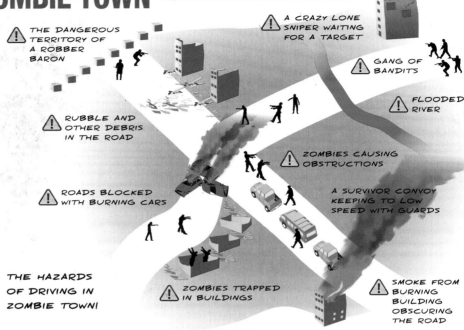

THE HAZARDS OF DRIVING IN ZOMBIE TOWN!

⚠ THE DANGEROUS TERRITORY OF A ROBBER BARON

⚠ A CRAZY LONE SNIPER WAITING FOR A TARGET

⚠ GANG OF BANDITS

⚠ FLOODED RIVER

⚠ RUBBLE AND OTHER DEBRIS IN THE ROAD

⚠ ZOMBIES CAUSING OBSTRUCTIONS

⚠ A SURVIVOR CONVOY KEEPING TO LOW SPEED WITH GUARDS

⚠ ROADS BLOCKED WITH BURNING CARS

⚠ ZOMBIES TRAPPED IN BUILDINGS

⚠ SMOKE FROM BURNING BUILDING OBSCURING THE ROAD

AUTOMOBILE TIPS

▶ Maintenance of your vehicle is essential – you do not want to either break down or run out of fuel with a few hundred ghouls watching you.

▶ Keep below 40mph (64 km/hr). Most accidents will occur at speeds above this so keep the speed down unless it's an emergency. Many roads will have become blocked so expect obstructions.

▶ Know the capability of your vehicle and adjust your driving style accordingly. Don't try taking your modern hybrid through a deep ford only to get yourself stuck in mid-river, with salivating zombies on each bank.

▶ Get in a regular routine of pre-drive checks – tires, battery, fuel and kit. Do these checks every time before you leave. Don't get caught out.

▶ If possible, go for a pre-1981 pickup in well-maintained condition. There is less technology on these older vehicles and you can still reasonably be expected to service them yourself. Get the latest four-wheel drive with onboard computer and you could find yourself stumped.

▶ Rotate your fuel supplies and add dates to cans so you can monitor usage.

▶ As a general rule, do not try to store more than 13 gallons (50 l) of flammable liquid in a residential location without some serious specialist storage facilities.

REMEMBER
F.I.T.B.O.W.

FLUIDS	Check your coolant and brake fluid levels and most importantly your washer fluid should be full as you will need to wash away blood smears.
INTERIOR	Check any Bug-Out supplies and you've got what you need for the mission.
TIRES	Inflated and carry a spare.
BASHERS	Onboard weapons for bashing.
OIL	Routine change and top up.
WINDOWS	Clear, with steel mesh secured in place.

⚠ **REMEMBER**

IF YOU ARE KEEPING A VEHICLE, YOU WON'T BE ABLE TO POP DOWN TO THE LOCAL GARAGE FOR REPAIRS. YOU WILL NEED A WELL-EQUIPPED WORKSHOP, WITH THE SUPPLIES AND SKILLS TO MAINTAIN YOUR TRANSPORTATION.

THE PERFECT ANTI-ZOMBIE VEHICLE

THE ZOMBIE KILLER

In 2010, a member of the Jordanian Royal family with strong links to the anti-zombie community offered a prize via his foundation to any engineer to come up with 'the perfect anti-zombie vehicle'. The rules called for the creation of a main vehicle, which should have the capacity to transport a group of survivors and be fit for general purpose use, and a smaller vehicle suitable for scouting or small-scale foraging. With the prize-money on offer, several major manufacturers entered and the winning designs, known as the 'Zombie Killer range' were announced in Amman in 2011.

Few survivors will have the time or resources to commission the building of one of these vehicles, but they are useful as you can take the ideas and implement them on your own vehicle. Think of these designs as the prototypes. Exciting developments such as the zombie scoop and firing platforms may be adapted onto your vehicle.

1 CHASSIS
Steel bar cage surrounding a padded cockpit for 4–5 fighters and supplies.

2 METAL BODY SCOOP
An adapted snow plough is welded to the front of the vehicle to push any run-down zombies up and to the sides of the vehicle.

3 SWIVEL MACHINE GUN TURRET
From this vantage point, a crew member can provide cover to any foraging teams or support by laying down fire into any hordes.

4 MOBILE MINI MORTARS
Smoke and sweat bombs may be fired at various angles from these small launchers.

5 TOUGHENED GLASS
The windscreen and side windows are special shatter-proof glass with optional darkening tint.

6 ESCAPE HATCH
Each model has an under vehicle escape hatch which can be used in emergencies.

7 LEG SLICERS
Each wheel is armed with extending metal blades which can be used to slice through zombie hordes.

8 EASY ACCESS
Two strong doors on each side so that an assault team can exit the vehicle swiftly and silently when on a mission.

9 STOWAGE AREA
Behind the seats there is an area for the stowage of weapons and foraged goods.

10 LIGHTING ARRAY
The vehicle is equipped with over 20 powerful lights, many of which can be directed from within the cabin.

THE ZOM 81E IS THE WORLD'S FIRST PURPOSE-BUILT ANTI-ZOMBIE VEHICLE

OUT AND ABOUT IN ZOMBIE TOWN

LONG-DISTANCE TRAVEL

Mass air travel will be one of the first casualties of the zombie outbreak. As countries rush to quarantine themselves and skilled pilots and mechanics scatter, it is unlikely that many will get off the ground in the months that follow. The military can be expected to keep flying for longer, but air travel on civilian jets, small private planes and most helicopters has a definite shelf life.

The hero of post-apocalyptic air travel will be the humble microlite. Flying high above the grabbing hands of the dead is a tempting prospect against the alternative of making your way through bumper-to-bumper cars, blocked roads and zombie-infested towns and for sure some survivors will make their escape in various light aircraft and helicopters. But, being realistic, microlites certainly won't be available for everyone and if you live in an urban area then car travel alone is going to be a challenge. Most short-range missions will be on foot – this will include any local foraging or scouting patrols. Cycles can be a useful option, but motorcycles tend to be too noisy – what you get in speed is often negated when the sound attracts all of the walking dead within miles of your location. However, long-distance travel, say 20 miles (32 km) or more will require much more planning and organization. And, believe it, that 20 miles through a zombie-infested land will be a considerable challenge.

LONG-DISTANCE TRAVEL THROUGH ZOMBIE-INFESTED AREAS

Longer journeys across zombie-infested areas, either on foot or in motorized transport, require skill and planning. Some journeys, such as a relocation to a more suitable long-term location, may be well-organized and structured while others, say following the collapse of your perimeter, may be more rushed and urgent. In the latter case, all survivors should make for one of the agreed Bug-Out locations, with their emergency supplies. Do not be tempted to take any more – for now, survival is the key. If your perimeter has fallen, don't be tempted to start packing up supplies – if it's chaos then just grab your Bug-Out Bag and go.

STEP 1
SCOUTING PARTY

Once the decision to move is made, use scouts to mark possible safe routes with spray paint and confirm the destination. Often working alone – these solo fighters may be able to secure sites en route for possible stops as well as checking the target location for zombies. Scouts should be light, fast and able to move quietly without attracting the attention of the dead. Typically, scouts should be fit and any experience in the armed forces is an advantage.

STEP 2
PACKING

Packing up supplies should be done in order of priority and according to how much you can reasonably carry. Allocate loads to different survivors and remember that your guards will need to be mobile so not everyone will be available for such duties. Never overload people and never slow down your guards. Budget for not more than 25 miles (40 km) per day if you are on foot but this figure will vary greatly according to the level of fitness within the group. The golden rule is never to overburden the convoy.

OUT AND ABOUT IN ZOMBIE TOWN
RIVERS AND WATERWAYS

Foraging by boat can be an invaluable way to safely explore new areas or secure those supplies, but although zombies can't technically swim, they can still represent a danger in the water. Millions will become infected in the zombie apocalypse and many rivers and waterways will become clogged with the undead debris of grabbing ghouls.

ZOMBIE-PROOF FLOATING PLATFORM

Some zombie survival experts argue that the benefits of living afloat are such that it is worth investing your resources in developing a floating refuge. In essence, it's a large raft that could be tethered in a lake or wide river and from which you could operate, using smaller boats to make foraging raids on the shore.

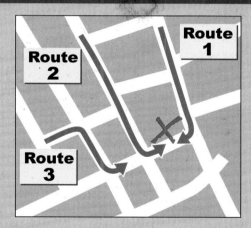

STEP 3
PLAN

Plan your main route carefully and have back-up routes in case you run into hordes of the dead. This is not a fighting mission – the objective is to reach the target destination with your survivors and supplies intact. Remember to budget to the speed of your slowest-moving vehicle or person. Ensure that you have temporary camping locations earmarked – this could be anything from an intact house to a tall tower where you can all huddle in safety on the roof.

STEP 4
PATHFINDERS

Use 'pathfinders' to track ahead of the main group. They will act as close scouts and check that routes are clear for slower vehicles. They will also monitor for any ambushes. During the actual move, keep guards on the flanks of the convoy. Try to keep a steady pace and do not stop to engage the dead unless you have to. Use a powerful rear guard, which can leave homemade bombs behind to deal with any 'tail of zombies' you might pick up.

During your convoy move, or any operation outside of your fortified base, it may be useful to use decoy techniques to draw the zombies away from your route of travel. Any noise or human commotion will attract the dead so sound can be a good decoy, but as zombies primarily hunt by scent, this can also be invaluable in sending the horde in the wrong direction by distracting them with bottles of sweat – though, of course, this scent must outweigh the amount being generated by your convoy as it struggles forward! It is most practical to keep the sweat in small grenade-like bottles.

GLOSSARY

apocalypse A great disaster; a sudden and very bad event that causes much fear, loss, or destruction.

barricade (v) To block (something) so that people or things cannot enter or leave; (n) a temporary wall, fence, or similar structure that is built to prevent people from entering a place or area.

cannibal A person who eats the flesh of human beings or an animal that eats its own kind.

corpse A dead body.

decomposition The process by which dead organic matter separates into simpler substances; decay; rot.

desiccated Dried up; drained of emotional or intellectual vitality.

gastric Of, relating to, or near the stomach.

ghoul An evil creature in frightening stories that robs graves and eats dead bodies.

metamorphosis A major change in the appearance or character of someone or something ; a major change in the form or structure of some animals or insects that happens as the animal or insect becomes an adult.

mutation A significant and basic alteration; change; a relatively permanent change in hereditary material.

outbreak A sudden start or increase of fighting or disease.

perimeter The outside edge of an area or surface; a line or strip bounding or protecting an area.

plague A large number of harmful or annoying things ; a disease that causes death and that spreads quickly to a large number of people.

post-apocalyptic The period of time and disastrous conditions that follow after an apocalypse; the aftermath of a massive and highly destructive disaster.

quarantine The period of time during which a person or animal that has a disease or that might have a disease is kept away from others to prevent the disease from spreading ; the situation of being kept away from others to prevent a disease from spreading.

siege A situation in which soldiers or police officers surround a city, building, etc., in order to try to take control of it ; a serious and lasting attack of something.

survivalist A person who believes that government and society will soon fail completely and who stores food, weapons, etc., in order to be prepared to survive when that happens.

symptom A change in the body or mind which indicates that a disease is present ; a change which shows that something bad exists : a sign of something bad.

transmission The act or process by which something, such as a virus, is spread or passed from one person or thing to another.

undead A creature that has movement, volition, and will, but is not technically alive, such as a zombie or vampire, and must feed upon the living in order to continue its existence.

virus The causative agent of an infectious disease; any of a large group of submicroscopic infective agents that are regarded either as extremely simple microorganisms or as extremely complex molecules that are capable of growth and multiplication only in living cells, and that cause various important diseases in humans, lower animals, or plants.

vulnerable Easily hurt or harmed physically, mentally, or emotionally ; open to attack, harm, or damage.

Center for Disease Control and Prevention's Zombie Preparedness Web Page
1600 Clifton Road
Atlanta, GA 30329-4027
Phone: 800-CDC-INFO (800-232-4636)
Website: http://www.cdc.gov/phpr/zombies.htm
http://blogs.cdc.gov/publichealthmatters/2011/05/preparedness-101-zombie-apocalypse/
What first began as a tongue in cheek campaign by the Center for Disease Control and Prevention to engage new audiences with
 preparedness messages has proven to be a very effective platform. It continues to reach and engage a wide variety of audiences
 on all hazards preparedness via Zombie Preparedness.

The Folklore Society,
c/o The Warburg Institute
Woburn Square
London WC1H 0AB, UK
Phone: +44 (0) 207 862 8564
Website: http://folklore-society.com
The Folklore Society (FLS) is a scholarly society devoted to the study of traditional culture in all its forms. It was founded in London
 in 1878 and was one of the first organizations established in the world for the study of folklore. The Folklore Society's interest and
 expertise covers such topics as traditional music, song, dance and drama, narrative, arts and crafts, customs, and belief. It is also
 interested in popular religion, traditional and regional food, folk medicine, children's folklore, traditional sayings, proverbs, rhymes,
 and jingles. Its aims are to foster the research and documentation of folklore worldwide, and to make the results of such study
 available to all, whether members of the Society or not.

Zombie Research Society (ZRS)
Contact: Mogk@ZRS.me
Website: http://zombieresearchsociety.com
Zombie Research Society (ZRS) was founded in 2007 as an organization dedicated to the historic, cultural, and scientific
 study of the living dead. The organization has grown to include hundreds of thousands of active members across the
 world. Its team of experts currently consists of a number of prominent authors, artists, and academics committed to the
 real-life research of zombies and the undead, as well as a core group of volunteers who handle the daily management of
 ZRS.

Zombie Squad, Inc.
P.O. Box 63124
St. Louis, MO 63163-3124
Email: chapters@zombiehunters.org
Phone: (888) 495-4052
Website: https://www.zombiehunters.org
Zombie Squad is the world's pre-eminent non-stationary cadaver suppression task force, committed to helping defend your
 neighborhood and town from the hordes of the undead. It provides trained and motivated highly-skilled zombie suppression
 professionals as well as zombie survival consultants.

Web sites

Due to the changing nature of Internet links, Rosen Publishing has developed an online list of Web sites related to the subject of this
book. This site is updated regularly. Please use this link to access this list:

http://www.rosenlinks.com/SZW/War

FOR FURTHER READING

Austin, John. So Now You're a Zombie: A Handbook for the Newly Undead. Chicago, IL: Chicago Review Press, 2010.

Borgenicht, David, and Ben H. Winters. The Worst-Case Scenario Survival Handbook: Paranormal. San Francisco, CA: Chronicle Books, 2011.

Brooks, Max. World War Z: An Oral History of the Zombie War. New York, NY: Three Rivers Press, 2007.

Brooks, Max. The Zombie Survival Guide: Complete Protection from the Living Dead. New York, NY: Broadway Books, 2003.

Emerson, Clint. 100 Deadly Skills: The SEAL Operative's Guide to Eluding Pursuers, Evading Capture, and Surviving Any Dangerous Situation. New York, NY: Touchstone, 2015.

Lonely Planet. How to Survive Anything: A Visual Guide to Laughing in the Face of Adversity. Oakland, CA: Lonely Planet, 2015.

Luckhurst, Roger. Zombies: A Cultural History. London, England: Reaktion, Books, 2015.

Ma, Roger. The Zombie Combat Manual: A Guide to Fighting the Living Dead. New York, NY: Berkley, 2010.

MacWelch, Tim, and the editors of Outdoor Life. How to Survive Anything: From Animal Attacks to the End of the World (and Everything in Between). San Francisco, CA: Weldon Owen, 2015.

MacWelch, Tim, and the editors of Outdoor Life. Prepare for Anything Survival Manual: 338 Essential Skills. San Francisco, CA: Weldon Owen, 2014.

Mogk, Matt. Everything You Ever Wanted to Know About Zombies. New York, NY: Gallery Books, 2011.

Piven, Joshua, and David Borgenicht. The Complete Worst-Case Scenario Survival Handbook. San Francisco, CA: Chronicle Books, 2007.

Piven, Joshua, and David Borgenicht. The Worst-Case Scenario Survival Handbook: Extreme Edition. San Francisco, CA: Chronicle Books, 2005.

Rawles, James Wesley. How to Survive the End of the World as We Know It: Tactics, Techniques, and Technologies for Uncertain Times. New York, NY: Penguin Books, 2009.

Wilson, Lauren, and Kristian Bauthus. The Art of Eating Through the Zombie Apocalypse: A Cookbook and Culinary Survival Guide. Dallas, TX: Smart Pop, 2014.

Wiseman, John "Lofty." SAS Survival Handbook: The Ultimate Guide to Surviving Anywhere. New York, NY: William Morrow, 2014.

AUTHOR'S ACKNOWLEDGMENTS

I hope you enjoy reading this book as much as we all did writing, designing and illustrating it. When we started, there were unbelievers working on the team, now we are all ready for the zombie apocalypse and slightly more paranoid than before. I want to thank my partners in crime Louise and Richard at Haynes for all their hard work and patience – both were last seen heading for their secure locations in Scotland. Also, to my wife for her tireless support as we spent weekends testing everything from crossbows to living in a sealed concrete bunker – see my website for details and more insanity – www.ministryofzombies.com. Finally, I want to mention all my family back in Ashford. I come from a close family – not in a weird or banjo-playing way – we just get along and this book is dedicated to them and my home-town.

⚠ WARNING!